Ghetto Girl Blue's *Speak the Unspeakable* is a work of poetic fiction based on her life and experiences as a foster child, a wife, a writer and an artist. All names, characters, incidents, and places are products of the author's memories and imagination combined for this ficticious literary presentation. Any resemblance to actual events, locales, or persons, living or dead, is coincidental.

Sale of this book without a front cover may be unauthorized. If this book is coverless, it may have been reported to the publisher as "unsold or destroyed and neither the author nor the publisher may have received payment for it.

A Ghetto Girl Blue New Age Blues Ensemble
Published by GGB Literary Entertainment, Inc.
Copyright 2000 by Jessica Holter

All rights reserved under International and Pan-American Copyright Conventions. Published in the United States by Jessica Holter, Founder of The Punany Poets, Oakland, CA.
GGB Literary Entertainment
360 Grand Avenue, #265
Oakland, CA 94610

All rights reserved. No part of this book may be reproduced or transmitted in any form or by any means, electronic or mechanical, including photocopying, recording or by any information, storage and retrieval system, without permission, in writing, from the author.

Grateful acknowledgment to artists, media, and performers who have assisted with advanced promotion of this and all material in association with The Punany Poets.
"Punany" and The Punany Poets
are registered Trademarks of Jessica Holter
Punany Logo is the sole property of Jessica Holter

Distributors contact us at www.thepunanypoets.com

ISBN 0-9700395-4-9

Cover design and illustration by Jessica Holter
First GGB Edition: May, 2000
10 9 8 7 6 5 4 3 2 1 0

Speak the Unspeakable

by Ghetto Girl Blue

GGB literary Entertainment, Inc

Ghetto Girl Blue

Table of Contents

8	Mostly it is Wet
10	Speak the Unspeakable
15	My Sister
16	Whichever Wind
17	She Says
18	Mama's Lil' Baby
21	You Say
22	Song Man Charade
23	Soul Glow Papa
24	Light Eater
26	If There is a God
27	Home For Christmas
29	Completely Chemical
31	I Loved a Man
32	Cinderella's Sober Vision
33	Travel a Brawd
35	Travel a Brawd, Pt II
37	Notha Way
38	Your Love is A Loaded Gun
39	Shame on the Wench
38	Last Chance Stew
39	It Ain't One Love
40	Blind Inside Her
41	Wreckless Abandon
43	Perfect Enemies
43	Think
44	My Hair and the King
46	Didn't Plan to Fuck
48	Birth of a New Breed
50	Dress Rehearsal
51	Love Ain't Suppose to Hurt
52	Soulution
54	Settlin' Down
56	Love Walk
57	Revolution of A Poet
60	The Master's Wife
62	The Gifted Ten

Table of Contents

64	No Hollidays for the Blue
65	The Sweetest Thief
67	Blue Black Jazz Daddy
69	The Whore Who Bleeds My Bloodtype
74	Never Less Than a Man
75	Milk Man
78	Ghetto Girls Don't Lactate
80	The Little Nigger Who Was
84	Sanctified & Satisfied
86	Their Souls Have Eyes
89	Simile
90	Once More for the First Time
93	Somebody's Somebody
94	Whore in this House
97	Sister's Wake Up Call
100	Black Words Soft Spoken
104	Shackles Don't Stop the Flow
106	No Such a Thing
107	My Brother's Keeper
108	Junkie Heaven
110	Antirevolutionaryexcuseism
111	Niggah They Call You
113	White Massa Fa' Toby
114	Would You Could You in a Boat?
116	Little Mary's Hippie Song
118	Alabi African
121	A Song For Old Souls
122	The Devil's Mass
124	Mythology of a Black Man
125	A Dick Witted Cop and His Wife
127	Jane Therese
130	A King, See?
131	My Sister, Sugar Water & The Ghetto Blues
134	Mostly Jane
135	Brandy: Me & You
136	Small Feats
138	Copy Cat Black
142	Hypothesis Now
143	My Blackened Heart
144	Young Gifted & Drunk
149	"The Caboose" Novel Excerpt
160	The Story of Blue (Writer's Biography)

Welcome to the mind of GGB...

Creator of The Punany Poets

Speak the Unspeakable

Dedication

To Life.
To Death.

To the struggle that is
between them.

Ghetto Girl Blue

Mostly it is wet.

mostly it is wet.
my mind, i mean
it is wet.
with the liquidation of your fantasies,
the baptism of blackmale prophecies,
big brother's logical fallacies,
about you.
about me.

he be thinkin we just be fuckin
but we believe truth without understanding her
she is clairvoyant, inherent,
telling...
when we listen

she is incensed by our secrets
compelled to spill herself
in our bed

my runaway kunta
did they wound ya?
hurtcha? raypya? burnya? take yo chil'ren?

they cut of your foot and you still runnin

to my bed for forgiveness

humm hmm, we understand one another
we just don't want to talk about it.

truth is one sexy bitch
let's have an orgy with her and her revelations

for the thought of you secreting intellectual, thoughtful honesty
inside of me

makes me wet.

makes my mind cum

over and over again until it hurts
i mean it...
really fucking hurts
like virgin fag ass
it hurts so good,
i know my heart should feel shame
but all i feel is my mind,
and mostly it is wet

we have both shed
in search of your dignity

mostly it is wet.

slick with the possibilities of what we could be
if we let go

Speak the Unspeakable

I'm just a girl
A lowly, lonely ghetto girl
Trying to survive in this
Not so forgiving "Man's World"
What do I know?
I'm just a female

All hail to sex unveiled
In seedy city streets
Love for every stranger I meet
All to build a castle for my king
King of Kings without a throne
Without a crown,
White man keeps him down there,
Looking to pussy wielding street soldiers
With Punany Dreams of
reparations
temporary love
for compensation
a path to Hades I prepare
as I dress my bed
for The Trick Slayer

slide in and hide
from my better mind
and pretend I am not dying
for a llittle while

(He cums before he calls)

He wants me so

Cuz I played it all out like
my king taught me to
Got him

sprung out on this good thing
buying time with a strung out bitch

kissing every place
the sickness don't show

But like the angel said
"I'm an honest ho"
and so I said
and
he knows

And still

(he cums befor he calls)

He wants me so

So I got to thinking, you know?

It may be, King Daddy
you wasn't completely honest with me
when you said what you said
to get me to do
what you wanted me to

You know
about the sum of my worth
how my parents didn't love me
how we were more than hustlers,
more than family
that we were a team
Like pimpin Bond
and Pussy Galore
Partners

Call a meeting
let's divide up these lesions
and get to work on living with this shit

cuz dying ugly is hard to do alone

But no, motherfucker
"You had to go"
just like my momma
cuz
I'm a scarlet ho
and you ain't got use for me no mo

Death has reared is ugly head
My life reels by in frames
Like fast Hollywood flicks

I watch myself but I don't feel
Menacing tricks
raping my innocence

My body Speaks the Unspeakable
still slightly silently
Each phrase is punctuated
With "Save me baby" pleas
As I bow before them on my knees
Blow intensly as they please

Death is coming
I can smell it in me

In search of
The love Sick One

Now he has come
and loves

(He cums before he calls)

he wants me so

History won't be undone
But victory will be won
And I will call it mine

As long as my body supplies
Bumps and grinds and lover's cries
I don't care how my body lies
If it can keep me
From dying alone
at the foot of the throne
I built; Hell will know King Daddy's guilt
God won't remember his name

On judgement day
What will he say?
"I taught her to walk the stroll"
"How to recognize a desperate soul"
"How to make a man a trick,
Who could lie, cheat and steal
for the thrills she supplies him with"

Beneath my sultry lips
Within my gyrating hips
Imbedded in my eyes
Even the cream on my
thighs is painful, shameful,
Perhaps unforgivable lies

ann Dick can find
only a man can forgive

No whore such as me
Would ever see
A man who'd make me his wife
But if I squeeze real tight
Whip it just right
He'll lay down his life
Pick up a knife
His weakness unleashed by my thriller in me
Compelled to become a killer for me

Through my stripes I've learned
Victory is not given, but earned

By the swift of mind

The Devil's been kind
To free me from my rage

I hate him
I resent his seed in me
I make him love me

I want to die soon
I want to die faster
I want you to die first

here he cums again, Daddy
The Trick Slayer

(he washed the blood from his hands)
(Looked in the mirror)
(Dried them)
(Crawled into my hiding place with me)

I don't miss King Daddy at all
just that way he had of willing me into anything

he tosses in his sleep
I hold him in duty
suck him in gratitude
knock him out with it

(I still got it like that)

I close my eye
and will my self to keep sleeping.

My Sister

I'm not a religious woman
But I know how to love
My sister
Don't want you to have to go to Jesus
Want you to build an alter on my soul and
Lay your burdens down
With Sister fellowship I will bear your cross
With a little help from our
Sisters
I'm not a religious woman
My mouth is too full of soul healing tales to chant
Nam myoho renge kyo
Into the mirrored belly of Buddha
For when I see your face
Distorted with pain
I have seen my reflection
When I nurse the wounds your lover leaves
Across Your heart; Your body; Your Face
I have healed my own .....wounds
And when you cry aloud at night
Thinking no one hears
Because Man's God
Has turned a deaf ear to
The Sisters
I am hoarse in the morning
Too hoarse, my sister
To pray to God
Too busy knowing how to love you
My
My
My
Sister
I know.... How to love you

Whichever Wind

She'll go whichever way the wind blows
She don't need clothes
She's happy in his arms
She don't need a home
She's so content to roam
Whichever way the wind blow
That Whichever Wind

She don't know
The lovin', true lovin, of a real man
The kind with a plan
To keep her safe and loved, to keep her strong
Got to keep her movin' on,
No settling down, no making connections
Her life is one sad song
Of empty rejections and midnight confessions
To God alone, to keep on sending
That heart mending Whichever Wind
That Whichever Wind

He steals her blessings all night long
Until she ain't got nothin left
Nothing for her child, nothin for herself
All that she has, is his, it's so sad
She's glad to find
The patience to keep waiting
For the next whichever wind, 'cause
When he's drunk or feeling bad,
Crazy, mixed up, stupid, mad
The night air cools her, whipped flesh
The night air cools her, whipped flesh

Keep on Coming Whichever Wind
Whichever Wind

She says...

She says she wants to be with *him*,
Though any man would do
First come, first serve
The old adage still reigns true
She says she needs her man to qualify her
Dignify her, magnify her
Would take a man who'd stand up tall
Or lay right down and die for her
She says she needs two loving arms
Around her even if it is a lie
She needs a man who loves her so much
It spills through his fists uncontained
She says it's just a bruise
And bruises they do fade
That he didn't mean it,
Wasn't trying to hurt her,
Won't do it again, cried when it was over
That he needs her to feel his pain,
Know his shame
That it's just fear of losing her
That's driving him insane
She says its just pain
And pain, it does go away
What is more, it makes making up
Soooo good the next day
The Next Day.... She Says...

Momma's Lil' Baby

so now you done got clean
you wanna save me?
Momma's little baby love strollin strollin...
you wasn't here when he said
he had love fa me
where was you back den
where was that pie inna sky hymn
I thought I rememba'd you sing
befo dem pipe dreams
read us a never ending story
like dem bible people
what neva did begat a clue
hard times had me missin' you
and findin you
in him

   he said he would
die a millions times if only I'd let him
if only he could
be with me forever
me his Ghetto Cinderella
he my ever true pimp
at first I didn't want to do it
He said at worst I'd
cry my way through it....

but afterwards... no words
to hurt or fake, but bread to break
a table to sup, my cup runneth over...

no curse, no omen, nothin' to show men
They ain't seen already nor did
I love you momma but don't chase me no mo' and
don't come after me too
nothin you kin do
and don't you be blue
no creed as true as that of the stroll
old woman be glad to know
yo' baby done grown
to a' honest ho
Momma's little baby love strollin' strolling
Momma's little baby love strolling tracks
Momma's little baby love hoin' hoin'
Momma's little baby ain't never comin back

'member when you useta
hit a' blazin' pipe torch
to whisk poverty 'way
t'da pie in na' sky betta day?
yet you say somebody usin' me
freedom be 'tween
me an them
no curse, no omen, nothin' to show men
they ain't seen already, nor did

A po'er day done hid
hin' dollar signs, shine bright like
your hot pipe light in small brown
summer night eyes an'
sizzling growling belly aching away
all night awake an' holdin' you shakin
beggin you to stay but
 you lef' me alone
trying to raise me now that i'm grown
my plight be da fruits you done sewn
 I did my best to never go hungry no mo
old woman you need to be knowin'

  your baby is well and your baby is happy
  with the daddy that got me t' hoin'
  don't cha worry y'self none
  it all be ova soon
  we be laughin' allis away
  you wit da pipe high
  me wit da sor' thigh
  what tingle wit herpe venom
   r'n'r
   one day well gett 'em
  in na pie inna' sky betta day
  cain't fret over where we goin'
  cause Lawd knows where we been
  May the church say amen
  May every Third eye
  Say Ashay

YOU SAY

You say I'm crazy —
I say it isn't true
My heart keeps whispering
Lies to my brain -
The more my heart breaks —
The more my love fades
Making little room
For my brain to tell the truth

You say I'm crazy —
You call me a fool
I must be crazy —
To be in love with you

You say I'm crazy —
How could I be so blind
Every time you kiss me —
I think you'll hit me
I flinch away - and you say -
You wonder why —
You say you're sorry —
Quick as you beat me
You say you're lonely —
But then you leave me
Gotta spend the holiday —
With the wife you left before -
She's got your baby
And she don't - ask for much more -

Trying to make some changes —
My life just stays the same
Long as you're in it
Won't be no winning
It's pain you're giving
Pretty soon I - won't be living —
You say I'm crazy
You call me a fool
I must be crazy
To be in love with you

Song Man Charade

I don't care about the
Money you've been making
I don't care about the
Females you've been fading
I don't care about the
Hearts you've been breaking
I don't care about the
Love you've been faking
I only want to save my soul
Tell me song man charade
You had it made but
On your way out of the door
Do you have a song
To let me know
Where do broken souls go
I'm not so bad
And not so good
That I should be hell bound or
Heaven ascending

Stop pretending to be
A song man for a little while
Telling gentle lies through
That charade you call a smile
I have no time to take a ride
or spend time saving
your song man pride
I'm a woman now,
Fighting grown up fears
I haven't time for song charades
I've dried all my little girl tears
My broken soul's torment
was the price I've paid
For participation in your
Song Man Charade
But one more thing before you go
Do you have a song
To let me know
Where to broken souls go

Ghetto Girl Blue & DJ Blackmon

Soul Glow Pappa

Soul Glow Pappa
Before there was Punany we were
Two spirits meeting
Molten together
Like hot lava love
Burning like the
Perm you used to comb through your hair
Soul Glow Daddy
We been ghetto Stupidstars
Forgot who we are
I'm a prodigal daughter of love
A runaway slave
In search of my old master
An empty grave
Waiting to be filled with ... home
Soul Glow Daddy
Be mine forever
Mine For real
From the tip of my
Cerebral cortex
To hot Sticky Punany Sex
The kind of Black Love
That brought your naps back...
Daddy, and I mean that sincerely
I hold you so dearly
In spite of all that we did and will do
I gotta a love for you
Truer than truth
More promising than youth
Sharper than hater's lies
It ain't between my thighs
It's the Sparkle in my eyes

The way you're
Fucking my mind...
Feels so good it must be a sin
Nail me to that cross again
Crucify this old time fixation to get
A glimpse of your glowing rainbow
extending me back home
To kiss with Boone's Farm scented lips
penetrating the night with our
unified soul as we roll fantisizing primer paint
is candy apple red and displayed on the sleek
body of a Porshe
Who the hell is she?
Niggah don't play me...
Instead of a bug
Don't be buggin young thang you
know your momma wants you home soon
but it's cool, I fooled her into thinking you were gay
daring the stars not to grant wishes
"you know you love somebody
or you're a drunk muthafucka when you..."
Relieve bodies of pee together
just pee together
In a city owned alley after curfew
a few minutes before
the cocks crow
is choked
disgraced and still the
crabs claw at the face
and all I want to do
is cry a river of ghetto tears
in your ghetto embrace
Ghetto... She's a raw bitch she
Strong as the bitch she made of me
would never deface
a love so *her*, so ghetto
won't stop for a Java
Soul Glow Papa
the before, the after, my friend
Soul glow daddy
Can we get Ghetto again?
Let's just
Get Ghetto Again

Light Eater

Even in the darkest night there glows
In the distance
The faintest of light
Months ago, even when it hid from me behind depression
and ingestion of the knowledge of Jane's heinous fate
and of the permanence of the absence of the Jamaican
Prince of the dreams of him she made mine
I could feel the pulse and the heat of light beckoning me to it
Begging me to live against my own will
To bask in its glow
Fate would have it's way and I would meet its glow
Emanating from the innocent eyes of my new born child
Promising me a new crystal clear future
Once I had a light of my own
It was brilliant and contagious
Now I am an eater of light.
I eat the light of my child that is new and full of the promise
I once possessed
I hope his light will continue to regenerate in the years to
Come as I am fed
I hope my experience and the love I have for my little one
will energize the light I must steal, replacing it with loving
examples he will be proud to follow some day

If There is a God

If there is a God
He will keep making me a strong
Presentable woman
So that a man will come
So that a man will want me
So that a man will mold me
With warmth and love
and discipline
and wisdom
Like clay
And He
will be
my new god

Home for Christmas

I'll be home for Christmas
On this she could depend
He left his family nearly a year ago
and made a home within her soul
Good loving all the time
Father to her child
Provider above his means
Let me be a man
Watch me make you a queen
I'll be home for Christmas he'd say
On this you can depend
She watched her independence pass
And fought the slow knowing in her mind
That the good times wouldn't last
The only hint of her existence

Was this old green couch
Nice, leather, kind to his feet
The only thing he let her keep
When he moved her into that house
Just around Thanksgiving
He started picking fights
Staying out all night
Sometimes many more
Her darting eyes
Her twisted face
Suggested his queen had forgotten her place
But what were her tears for?
He wanted to know
As he kicked and bit her
Between the moments he stole to cuss
You are after all my queen and

I'll be home for Christmas
On this she could be sure...
An afternoon tour
Through his pager files
The pictures all to recent of his
Abandoned family all aglow with smiles
Full of laughter they seemed to be
Hugging long lost daddy
Beneath a Christmas tree...

I'll be home for Christmas
She could plainly see
As she dried her eyes and packed his clothes
And tried to be a big girl while she
Bid him farewell home
She listened while he told her
She was trying to destroy his family
She was a whore, a Jezebel
Trying to see him burned in hell
But like I told you, I'll be home for Christmas
On this he had no doubt
Then he opened the door
Tossed her things
And put her and her child out
She watched his wife and children move right in
Peered into the windows while they were sleeping
Never saw her madness creeping
Never caught it's scent from
Her concrete home in spying distance
Just across the street
She rocked her child and bid Happy Holidays
To the strangers that she'd meet
Who'd break a dime and take the time
To listen to her Christmas rhyme
Thank You, Thank You ma'am and Merry Christmas too
Make sure that your home and man really belong to you
I never knew how much four walls
Could really mean to us
Until this concrete haven
Welcomed us home for Christmas

Completely...Chemical

I want to play where only God's have been.

Ain't it fine?...
Spending time this way
You up there
Me, way down here
Us so far away
We, so meant to be spent
Completely...chemical.
Like animal attraction man
Like, I love you
God Damn you,
Like, I don't understand you!
You make me sick bitch!
Is you bleedin' or what?
You are fucking tripping! Like, Mad Max
Way beyond the Thunderdome
you Dig?

I want to play where only God's have been.

You are fine as fuck, Mothafucka
(watching you walk from the bed to the dresser into the bathroom)
squad, sit, piss
Even that shit is sexy
but you don't
as far as I know, you never do
anything
anything
anything
to defoul my sensibility of you

Tell me what to do
with your body

your ass.

Your ass makes me manic, wanna touch it
No, Rub it, softly, no, ok, well it's like this
With two fists full of your ass in the grip of my hands
I an incensed with control

What to do
What to do
What to do with so much ass?

Like it
Kiss it
Beat it with wild lashes of my tongue and face
Go down below
Is that your asshole?
It's perfect as your hips
As your perfect lips
Tight and tiny
Perfect as a virgin
And I
I want to play where only God's have been.
Let me feel your back bend

A completely chemical reaction to your ass descends.

I Loved a Man

He use to listen to me
My woeful cries of poverty
Haunting me
Daunting me
Calling to me to die someday soon
Rap myself in God's bosom
Forget the troubles of this world
Hope God forgives me for
Coming to him before
I lived out the plan he had in store
I loved a man
Placed him so high
I wanted to die
When he was gone
So wrong was I
To love a man
Place him so high
I forgot all about God
But God forgot me not
Today my man is gone
I must stand alone
And try to atone
Greet fate as it unfolds
Place my back to the cold
Long no more for streets of gold
Sweet chariots taking flight
I'm standing alone
And find a light
In a lonely place
Where all around me is black
Trying to remember
That God's got my back

Cinderella's Sober Vision

Once upon the Ghetto
You lived in the throne of my heart
In a twinkling of your intoxicating eyes
I was transformed
Where indoor flea market rags
Once scratched my supple longing flesh
Versace's linens and Betsy's silks
Now drape over my still longing heart
I thought your money equaled love
You mistook my love for weakness
What a fool I used to be
But this is Cinderella's sober vision
And now my soul is no longer for sale
Over my lips you poured Crystal
Laced with some magic potion for love
And while you ran around boy
Ran around boy
I was intoxicated by something
In your flash
I stood dumb and dazzled in the door
As you ran through boy
Packing for weekends away
I took the clip full of money
For my shopping therapy
Trying to fill the void
Your absence left inside of me
What a fool I used to be
This is Cinderella's sober vision
And now my soul is no longer for sale
Sitting at home, draped in designers signatures
Aching for your touch
Your smell
Your love
No where to go
And no man to take me
If there were
What part of the game is this?
I'm not a come up
At least not anymore
So please sugar daddy
Take it all back
And give me back my soul

Travel A Brawd

Part One
what an honor you thought
nubian hands handing you
nubian musk incense and
new black nubian body oil
his nubian lips speaking of his nubian
god and of peace within
but without the ghetto
before you know it
your doubting
you ever knew anything at all
cept dreams of being in them strong nubian arms
and becoming a new being

blessed to walk two paces behind him
suckle his little ones and
those of the community sisters
who share the responsibility to
never allow the evil spillage of his seed upon the ground

you dropped freedom at the incense stand
in the indoor flea market when you bargained
a nubian man with nubian musk incense and oil
and nubian power and nubian passion that made your heart toil
like alabaster fingers in nubian soil
foiled by words and visions and nubian community missions
that gave you new comprehension
of what was true ascension
him...
climbin' every mountainous yam of your kitchen
suckin' dry every chicken bone
leavin' them on the plate
you...
keep babies quiet don't give up all your milk though
when the game is over he'll be your kingdom comin' lover
a forty five minute brother
you painin' every tenth inch of it
cover your head and don't say shit
off streets he said he took you
donned in rocks from swapmeets...

Nubian made new being
made a queen of a brawd
don your weave worn head with dread of all not spawn of his law
i mean my king, don't get me wrong
i've been trying to tell her what an honor it is to
have been desired at all
to walk two to ten paces behind you, suckle your children
and to be blessed with the honor to share the responsibility to
never allow the evil spillage of your seed upon the ground
but somehow she ain't down
talking something bout how she work
and take shit off the white man everyday
that ain't no way she had time to be stroking
no sorry ass, need a scapegoat
hate whitey but quick lick that soft as skin
when it's garnishing a chick
brother
anyway
i came to say
sister's be strong inffin you do got or don't got a place to stay
a man to pay
your bills
keep servin' thrills ghetto
style
u know Punany run the long mile
cause he wanna introduce you to his
lawd
who live down a long road
he don't even travel
a brawd.

Travel a Brawd
Part 2

he wants to travel a brawd
see the world
through a Queen's eyes
he heard she be wise
and she be strong
even on her own
she raise kids
two or three of his brothers
one or two of his
he wants to travel a brawd
see the world
through a queens eyes
without comprehension
of the blood on her thighs
ancient circumcision
induced shuffle of her step
muted cries fall on deaf village ears
pass the whiskey
pass the pipe
pass the knife
old Woman Moses done
stitched too tight
limp men
simpin
cut the virgin open
you may be use to
all my freaky poems
but
i'm schoolin you tonight
sho' you right

but he knew he was wrong
to wanna
travel a brawd
see the world
through a queens eyes
never
wiping the blood from her thighs
while plunging *deeper and deeper*
in the spoils of her labor
and she bett not cry
i-i-i-i-i--I-I-ke!
don't get none on ya
it burns disco inferno hot
passion pouring from every pour
yet he's ignoring the root
in search of nappy loot
he wants to travel a brawd
see the world
through a queens eyes
catch that pigeon catch that pigeon
nooooowwwww
gentlemen on standby travel are hereby notified
of cancellation amendment
1865-2000 zero zero party over you're out of time
shake the fiend
let this poet jester
confess yeah, wake the queen
to reality of self love
for no one got hol on *pleasure principle*
the heart will drown in its own blood
when love is not reciprocal
so if you savor the sauce of a brawd
yet your looking for a queen on 9 0 & East 14th
she went home to the lord
she god , we god, we got we got we got
what you need
for fee god
many a turbin donned time ago
that bowing, covered, clitless shit
could never survive the ghetto

Speak the Unspeakable

Notha Way

I's a nother way coming
It coming fas', dat shit is slightly tight
No bougeouisdom necessary
Welfare & penitentiary pimpin' dairy
from a WIC tittie
an' city streets is scary to even the oldest g
soap box preachers got no cheeks lef' t' turn
n' baby got ADD from the way our money burn

So Niggahs, brotha's and nothers
Is gatherin' drug and GA funds
sellin' guns and Pun by the ton
gamblin' winnin's 'n
checks, to bet on a new black millennium

Done hushed da green envy tinted blues
trade sneakers fa' walkin' shoes
getin' on the bus, took the caddy and park'd it
bettin 40 acre's on 'da stock market!

great day in 'na morning
whatchusay!
I feel a notha' way
it's the illigimate master's son
raisin' pens not fists
black power without a gun
free from trivial idiom
gettin on
bettin on
a new black millenium

Your Love is a Loaded Gun

Your love is a Loaded Gun
How can you say you love me
When your love is a loaded gun
Like a snake in a rose garden
I am your prey
You are stinging me
Your love is a Loaded Gun
Biting me
Your love is a Loaded Gun
Fighting me
Your killing me softly with bullshit..
Your love is a Loaded Gun
And I've come too far to go out like that
...Just when
My rough edges had been smoothed over with trust
With tenderness
What is this mess
Confess you don't love me
You just want to fuck me
If this is the case
If this is the deal
Lights out
Curtains down
No audience for applause
Just fuck me in the dark and
Keep it real
But don't say you love me
Even if it's how you think you feel
Cuz,
Your love is a Loaded Gun

SHAME ON THE WENCH...

i live in a house of words. somebody forgot to wipe their feet before coming in. somebody put stank feet on my table. i serve proverbial verbs on crystalized dreams and truths and deaths and horrors in black and bloody stew that mirrors image. somebody stank feet on my bathroom floor, ashy hand clutch porcelain god singing shame on the wench! shame on the wench! take her house from her.

Bind Inside Her

Ever wonder what is on her mind?
    She couldn't see you coming
    In all ways looking behind
Seems.
    through tender midnight blows, her body would find what her heart could not know
Never.
    do mind to take the time to see into her crimson mind; her bluenote lows; the ups and downs her story goes
Hope.
    she'll look up one day and see you for the very first time
Nevertheless.
    you find what you've been searching for all your life
Salvation.
    in her silence
Kingdom.
    in her obedience
Regeneration.
    in her submission
Think.
    you have found what you're looking for once you're inside it
Trust.
    It only seems to fill you for a little while
Like a pedafile
    You come up with Short Eyes
Blind.
    Inside her, Blind. Blind Inside Her
Nevermind.

Reckless Abandon

Ah
Ah
Ah
How can you breath like that
Relaxed
When shit is moving so fast?

That's what you trive on
That's what you live off
Your reckless abandon is my inspiration
I should have understood this,
by the way you work a stickshift
and hadled a curve ball
You were a reckless girl

Then how come you can't be wreckless in our love?

I never want to lose you
And I don't want to leave you
If we abandon anything
Let's abandon wrecklessly

Our fear

And if I say I want to be your wife
Why can't I free my fear to hear me
Thinking that you'll crave a man
When all you've done is believe in me?
And for all my wreckless talk
My fancy high step,
 My bold walk
 Why can't I be wreckless in our love?

Ah
Ah
Ah
I never want to lose you
And I don't want to leave you
If we abandon anything
Let's abandon wrecklessly
Our fear

Perfect Enemies

Baby looked so good
Down on his knees
Sweetest mouth
Girlish pout
(Open girls
Know what I mean)
Turned so foul
I never thought
He would stand up to me

Once we loved
So
Certainly
Perfectly
Now we 're perfect enemies
Now we are Perfect
Enemies
As perfect as we were
In our love

Think

Think
Long
Think
Wrong
Think,...
But think
And do it
For yourself

My Hair & The King

I woke up early this morning expecting a hair client. A gentle knock on the door, my soul.
Hello? Come in my king. I wanted to wash his feet in oils of old... but my hair...
Oh,
My Hair!
Knots too short
Too modest in length and texture to be called strands - broken and beaten from perms, color, stress, life as the ghetto defined it... the white woman's image on the pedistle just outside my grasp compelling me to reach to magazine racks for the image of my perfection... I could not.
A master in my house, and I could not.
My shame compelled me not to speak but to drop to my knees, to bow my head and mutter like a slave.
"I will not be able to wash your feet today."
He sat between my knees, looking out upon the pictures of my children, placed on boxes of various shapes and sizes, decorated as only 3, 4, 5, 6 and 7 year-olds can express themselves.
...As I twisted his locks.
"Funny", I said.
You don't look like any of your pictures.

Didn't Plan to Fuck

Bright as the california sun
I was
Clever to a fault
No doubt I should have been in school
Never should have taken the bus
Crossed those tracks
been anywhere close
to Sobrante Park
But there I was
15 year-old plump n rip fa pickin's
trying to keep a twenty year-old man's interest
Wanting to test my power
To make a man
Want me...for me?
Maybe
But is was clear to me
I didn't plan to fuck.
"When Lois finds a man he's gon' really love her", I could hear Momma say as I crossed the threshold.
"When you find a man
He's gon' think you think you're half way cute
and he'll beatchoo!"
He wore a robe
Freshly showered
Watched a video tape of Charlotte's Web
A movie he had rented from the video store I worked at in Foothill Square
Who after all could resist a featured
Soulbeat Entertainment Television commercial actress?
He was cute
Kind of innocent looking
Before he did his Jekyl and Hyde thing
Caste me from God's garden screaming

"I didn't eat the snake's fruit, He forced it into me!"
or
rather Ebonically into the perpetrator's imagination
"I didn't plan to fuck"

He just shoved it into me until
I could feel my insides shoved aside
My spine carried waves of shock and pain to my brain
But
Every 2nd hour or so
He'd inquire about my comfort, my hunger
Ease my fear with his tongue delved into places
I didn't even wash regularly
Then force his tongue into my mouth
Nothing is as distinct
As the taste of ones own blood...

Moral?

There seldom is one...

A fool learns from his own mistakes
A wise man
From the mistakes of others

The Birth of A New Breed

Verily, verily I say unto the
The righteous can not see me
I am half dead
One foot in the pulpit
The other in the grave
I came not to save the righteous
For they are not in need
I thirst to give
I long to feed,
My rhythm, my rhyme, my art, my song
I am the birth of a New Breed

Born of a regenerated womb
Met my first death on the slave ship
On the dawn of the third day
arose from the tomb
Unsaved souls jumped from the boat
Long before they reached shore
I embrace their pain
Sometimes, I think my third eye's blind
Like Mary Magdeline at the well, well I
See myself at Jesus' feet
They bathe in oil and annoint me
Dread locked in spirits embrace, I trace

The nails in His hands,
The blood on His feet
I'm Sampson, I wash them
With the redlocked power in me
Till my soul can see
the ancestors, dead hero's
haunting me
Billie sings of weeping willows
I cry to sleep in stranger's pillows
Alex wrote of finding roots
I rhyme of losing mine
I lay me down 'neath a lynch tree
Place pen to scroll
Watch the love bleed, I am
Dead alive,
yet, my soul survives
The rhythm, the song the art and the rhyme, see
I know yall can't hear me
Just don't fear my seed
I am
The Birth of a New Breed

Dress Rehersal

Dearest Friend,

      I was so happy to hear from you the other day. I found myself smiling and wanting to say, "I miss you boy, where have you been?" But before I could, you were announcing your wedding. I was dreading the words that followed...the same judgemental tyrades that keep my phone calls at bey. It's funny how those you love most can make you feel so very empty inside. When love has you open as wide as I was, there is no place big enough to hide in, no thing nourishing enough to curb the hunger pangs.

      It wasn't very long ago that you were professing your love for me, and though it might be that you've chosen another, I wonder how you can love her, when you're thinking of me? What I mean to say is, why is it you care who I bring to your wedding? Suggesting It need be my man. I thought you could understand, above all others, what, if anything, and who, if anyone, I am. I ain't the kind of girl who plans; I just kind of saddle up...ride the tide of emotion. Sure maybe it's nothing to be boasting about, but I seldom leave a doubt to put the truth of my marriage to freedom asunder.

      You are so quick to judge, yet I never held a grudge about the woman who spends up your ends, the way you shamelessly came at my friends, or even the night you busted out in hoop earings. Let us not pretend, this betrothment is more than an experiement, for tis the efiminent hint that that kept our relationship level at best. Though you don't possess the wherewithall to stand hand in hand with a man at the alter, I would never front you off and bring my woman to bear witness of this pretense. Just you remember this...My love is real, it never sleeps, yet it never forgets. Your soul and mine are for ever submersed in memories that all at once precede and supercede logic, plans or pressure. Look to the sky where you hear the pastor's words and remember, for better or for worse it was the wild chick who got you set for your dress rehersal.

Your Friend

Love, Ain't Supposed to Hurt

Love
Ain't supposed to hurt
Love Love
Ain't Supposed to hurt

I guess I should have
Listened to my momma
"Don't love a man, who
Don't love his momma
Got no respect for
Saints up above him
Got to let a ho be ho
Don't just apply to
A Woman
Love
Love
Ain't supposed to hurt
Love Love
Ain't Supposed to hurt

Ouch!!! Uuugh!
"Baybee, wait!"

> *All the things that attracted me to you*
> *Are in her, of her*
> *I loved her once. She beat it out of me.*
> *Beat respect for my father into me.*

"You said you wuzn't gon't hit me no more!"

Soulution

He's my daddy type
Cause he found me
Before I was ripe
Turned me into a real woman
Despite all the hype about virtue
Opened me up
Body and soul
Till no other brother would do
Like my Daddy Type
Some Kind of Freudian Hype
Got me feeling like
The more I know him
The more I love myself
I'm trying to keep up with all the love
And all the
Fortified game
He's filling me with
Give up your love girl
Without shame
Someday you'll make a name
For yourself
But until then
I've got the soulution to our
Financial destitution
Brotha's will come
And they will surely go
Sex is only sex; don't try to make it love
And when it's done
All you should be thinking of
Is how cash for ass
Will help you advance
To whatever level to which you aspire
My daddy Type could always
Take a simple thing
And make it higher
Oh, how I admired
His wisdom
I was his willing pupil
His dedicated victim

His subject to study and mold
Left no fantasies untold
No inch of my body unsold
This story is old
But still it's true
All I can do is tell it
So another child lover
Can recognize a daddy type before
It's everlasting too late
See my Daddy Type
Was a hype, a drug abuser, a user
A common needle pusher
Pushing me into the streets
To supply his habit
Every penny I was saving,
Every dream of havin' babies,
Every fantasy of moving
Away from the street
Worked their way through his veins
With a little reality check
Payment for all the lives
He turned out I suppose
Or all the daughters
He turned into hoes
Guess it's how life goes
How could I know?
You reap what you sow
When I never had a
Real Daddy to teach me
A hot shot got my Daddy Type
Before the check got cashed
But now I have assumed his debt
People think I am wrong
For being true to the stroll
But I keep tellin' them
It's all I know
Despite the fact I got AIDS
Game states
You gotta Let a Ho be a ho

Settlin' Down

How can you say you don't love me
And kiss me the way you do
Below the waste
and above the haste of
Our daily rituals

You go to work
Then, you work it out
I
Pick up the kids
Then, we get down

With every stroke of tenderness
You lay my soul to rest
I close my eyes and wallow
In the beauty of this scene
Hold on tight and swallow
My pride... Can leave me hollow
Won't worry bout tomorrow
Know what the world has to offer
Walt Disney won't grant blacks these
Story book fantasies of love, unconditional
Our is one-dimensional
Some blacksploitation drama commencing
Tonight in my house where I refuse to be alone
Called "Survival"
Daddy this woman is grown
Believe I have you here on loan

You know the song
All day long
I think about my baby?
Well, it just don't remind me of you.
But honey baby, sugar boo
Love ain't got the stamina
To survive the feel of you

Honey baby sugar boo
You feel so very good to me too
If the world was flat
I'd fall off the edge
Just to get one taste of you

Maybe one day you'll come around

To feeling the way that I do
But for now
I guess I'm just settlin' down

Love Walk

You are his queen
Elevated by his always increasing
Devotion
You are
The spine of His Story
The pulse of his love
Lay the Cadence
Of this love walk
Striding and striving
Spirits intertwining
You take the lead
Where you go
He will surely follow
Guided by the unfaltering
Motion of your essential thickness
He pours libations
Over the full swell of your hips
Calming his deep thirst
And breaks bread at your altar
Though the roads seems
Sometimes unending
You are driven forward
By his loyalty to his queen
and to his craft
Respect and expectations
The vision you share
He is the dream at your feet
Tread gently Nubian Queen

Revolution of a Poet

Say sista?
How much is it gon' cost you
To lend me your ear?
Brotha man?
What's the price for me to share
A slice of my life
Over this mic?
And just how many revolutions I got to start
To keep the applause coming?
How long are you going to keep the padlock
On my panties before you will grant me
The right to heal myself
Like Tupac, chill myself
With vicarious life of poetic psalm
Like Sonia I write
Like Sonia I do so
So I don't have to kill anyone
When I heard her words
Resounding through my mind
With the force of my own voice
I was shocked to hear them
I laughed to hear them
And was soothed to feel them
Wrap themselves around
My kind of fear of death
I ain't Martin been to the mountain top
Ain't fearing any man Luther
Seen the promised land King
Ain't ashamed to say
I fear death
But then I ain't subscribing
To a school of thought
That eases that sort of thing
I fear death; I do
Much the same way as
I feared the tippy pausin'
Eel skin squeak
Of my daddy's shoes

As he crept into my room
Lay atop of me spewing
Contradicktions
To the Christian stewardship
Rhetoric that first hipped me to
The difference between
Givers and takers
Talkers and doers
Fighters and the beaten
Ghetto Cinderellas and Drinking Dead Janes
And all the women in this room
Loving daddy's incapable of knowing the difference
Between
Loving a girl child and abusing her
Loving a woman and fucking her
Creating shame and fits of rage
His deaf ear fell on my kicking and screaming soul
as he dragged my limp body to a place
wear sun, moon and stars are never cast
Distorted lies,
threatening eyes, my tender thighs
Spread wide
Sex and death don the same mask
and love and war are the same
Thief in my temple of Innocence
Using this, Abusing this , Confusing this
Til only the devil remembered my name
then he adds blame to my shame
forsaking womanhood
with "Oooh, God damn you baby girl...
God Damn you for looking so good!"
The only daddy I've ever known
Killed me a little bit more each time
His sweet deacon minty tongue slipped
Into my speechless mouth
You'd better not never tell nobody but
Nobody but, Nobody but,,, Who?
Would listen to a Ghetto Girl Blue
Caught in red tape raptures
Whose only answer was another
Fostered, doctored, fake ass, getting paid family
Use the term loosely

The pad became my sister,
The pen my mother
The tape recorder, my brother
The news paper my ministry
And so I writeFreedom of words blew breath
Into me until I was revived
And now Punany saves my life
Keeping me alive, maybe save someone else's life
A little rhyme at a time
So to all the third eye
Motherfuckers
Hating on my kind of fear of death
Hating on Punany yet loving GGB
Still not understanding me
Don't even own a gun or even
Possess a permit
Talking about Revolution
Revolution
Revolution
That's pure Rhetoric
Revolution that's pure rhetoric
Telling me
Don't you talk about Punany
Don't you talk about Punany
Don't talk about Punany!
Well fuck me!
For wanting to make
Love ... Not war
And so I write, and so I write
Like Sonia Sanchez,
I write
So I don't have to
Kill anyone

The Master's Wife
For Dwayne Wiggins, Ghetto Hero

Love bows
To furious rage
In a curious cage called the ghetto
Wielded by clinched fists
Overseer's night sticks
Cocked gun...choke
Hold me for a little while
As if I had not been sold to serve in the big blue house.
Alone in a concubine's suite, there she sleeps in a casket of glass
Perfection untouched untested
Sound
Proof
Where is the music? Confined concubine hips can not sway
In the way of ancestors
While they lay for a Master in blue
She be so beautiful so fair, he will keep her near
Like trees that fall and make no sound
When no one is around to hear
Is beauty *beauty* if it is unseen?

You shattered the glass with your chains
Ran like a slave
Humming prophetically "she could never be me"
But you can't give me what I need
When all the glass had fallen
I sent my dogs to catch you
You returned battered, bruised, yet stronger for it
Together unseen, the world slumbers
I want your hands about me
But having surpassed the physical we mystically
Made love mentally
Infecting me with desire to live again
Injecting danger into swollen wanton hips
Sucking venom from cursed lips

Which no longer beg for, but live of and in freedom
Why should we run away?
My blood is the putty on the walls, foundation of master's name
We should not run away.
We should run to his bed
And fuck in his bed like savages
Like savages
And watch his blue house burn in
Our after glow
My hero
Under Master's hand
Runaway king
You, croon the song of Billy,
For I, The Master's Wife
Under Master's hand,
Again
We should not run away.
We should run to his bed
And fuck in his bed like savages
Like savages
And watch his blue house burn in
Our after glow

The Gifted Ten
....for the blackened burdens

There's nothing you can't say to them
Little they wouldn't do to please you
No place or need for you to run and hide
No one could ever push you aside
Nothing on this earth and nothing above
Could ever keep you from their love
   Even as they flourish in prosperity
   Wallow in iniquities, are banished to poverty
   Locked up and lock out of life as we know it
   They love the blackened burdens
   We the People get heavy sometimes
   It hurts like hell to lift us
   There is salvation in the soldier friends
   The sister's and brothers I call the gifted ten

They be the dark and lovely kings and queens
Still struggling to understand
Who is the dreamer? And where he been?
By any means necessary, who shot him?
The gifted 10 percent that keep us lifted
   So hater's beware, don't you never dare
   To call no coppa's 'cause the momma's and poppa's of
   This love revolution are screwing with your security
   If true love is scaring you, cause it's daring you to be real too
   Then they can lock us all up and throw away the keys
   But they won't find us on our knees
   Begging Uncle Sam Please........
   Cause no prison bars are strong enough
   No hustler is hard enough
   No dope man's cash is long enough
   No conspiracy is real enough
   No censorship could chill enough
   No third eye is wide enough
   No politics could lie enough
   No grave they dig is deep enough to keep my message from my peeps
   No bullets could pop loud enough
   No klansman could be proud enough to stop the
   Soldiers who told you
   To "keep your head up" and to "free your mind"
      and that we got to fight the powers that be

                    Keeping us victims of ourselves
Don't fear them, just hear them
and holler "I'm black and I'm proud"
 So what's up now?
With revolution raising fists without confusion
The new world order ain't no illusion
            So what you gonna do son?
            If your mouth is closed and your fists are down
            Guess you're just part of this institution
            Though I can feel your blues, still I choose
            To join the gifted soldier ranks
            And give thanks to the powers that be making us stronger
            No longer welfare recipients, liars, thieves, whores and drug dealer killers
            Not thrill seekers of the night but truth seekers in the light,
            soldiers in the fight
            The rebirth, baptized in ghetto fire
            Now Dark and Lovely kings and queens
            Still struggling to understand
            Who is the dreamer? And where he been?
            By any means unnecessary, who shot him?
            Gifted 100 percent keeping ourselves lifted
            Keeping ourselves lifted

No Hollidays for the Blue

We are the Blue people
Red, White and Blue
Blue. The color of our discontent
Sky Blue
High high high
Sky high
And still we are Blue
Black and Blue
Blue-Black
Sad and Blue
Gay and Blue
Rhythmically
Rhythmically
Rhythmically Blue
Effortless grace finds haven in
the unified soul of
the colorfully oppressed
"The blues ain't nothin' but a pain in your heart
When you got a bad start"
No Holidays for the Blue....
No Holidays for the Blue....
The Dead and Blue

The Sweetest Thief

Take your time sweetness
I'm always calling you that
'Cause that is how
I know it can be
Sweetness spilling from
Your lips, your tongue
That powerful part of you
From which promises are hung
From deep inside of you
To deeper inside of me
Coating that latex respect
In a long vibrating stream
Of sticky bitter sweetness
That I long to taste
Would savor, sugar flavor
Of my lover, familiar stranger
If only times were safer
Long after we have peaked
And I lay in the slick pool of
Responses to your touch, your kiss
Shaking, speechless
Quivering, speechless
The calm before the storm
Fantasy is pure bliss.....

Your sweetness chisels through
The ice walls of my heart
Stealing every doubt about love
Implanting a fantasy song
When in the midnight hour
You arise my heart still croons forget-me-knots
Even as you don your quivering, speechless,
Shaking, speechless pager
Empty kiss me on the forehead
Say you'll "catch me later"
Your mind void of the temple you robbed blind
Through the night
It is but the midnight hour
Yet a new but familiar day
Heart in stereo
Fantasy song ceases to play
The sweetest thief I've ever known
Speechless
But there's a song
Somewhere in there
The Sweetest Thief
I've ever known

Blue Black Jazz Daddy

Don't sugar coat my blues
Jazz Daddy I wanna be down
I was down so long till down didn't mean a thang
I was down so long till down didn't mean a thang
Then Jazz Daddy came, washed me in his
Blue Black Rain, Blow me down Jazz Daddy
Down just ain't the same
Finger dancing on the base of me
Chords tuning, deeply crooning
GGB, What's My Name?
My body responds....
Just a girl who is ghetto free
Roll out the red carpet for
Blue Black Jazz Daddy
To plant me in dangerous lands
That can fertilize my blues
Don't sugar coat my blues
Freak the bass once more
Like it was the first time
Blue Black Jazz Daddy I wanna be down
Blues raining, growing me down
In fertile rhythms
Never cry no mo' 'bout goin' down
Down is where I want to be
Thump it Daddy and hear this body squeal
Course and crude, raw and real
Make no apologies,

have no diplomacy
Freak sound til time stands still
As hard as steal
As natural as your dreads
Lock me in an embrace with
Knowledge of myself... Epiphany is true blue
Can you feel her? You're the only one
She can't come ... Unless you tell her to
Riiight here.....Riiight now....Right On
Now you've got it, Rhythmically Freaky
Blue Black Jazz Daddy Talk to me
I was down so long till down didn't mean a thang
Drowning in them happy jazzy rifts till I couldn't breath
but I could hear
Somebody saying don't worry be happy
Naw, Jazz daddy
Make my jazz down dirty and nappy
Make my jazz the blues ...Make my jazz the blues
Make my jazz....The Blues

The Whore Who Bleeds My Bloodtype

To Roni Sister, Sister: On My Voice Mail

Where is my thief?
Where is the gangbanger
Where is the hype
Give me the whore
Who bleeds my bloodtype...

She called me to say
Ain't no way she could associate with Punany
I can't blame the unknowing
But even God doesn't accept ignorance
I don't know you like that, so I wonder
If a backstreet never knew your feet
A back seat; your ass?

When you can sweet talk
A shamed brotha into
sparing your tender body
From his victim recoil
Till he's ready to release you
Then suddenly, like Jeckyl and Hyde
He has a change of heart
Pinning you, pissing in you, then kissing you....
Nurses the wounds
Of your ripped apart ass
And bleeding pussy ... pussing heart
But you still find a brand new start...

When you can find fresh air to breath
While society farts
Government cheese fueled gas
From it's welfare ass in your face
And listen to the woman you thought was your mother
complain that she ain't been paid enough to keep you...

When you can find sleep enough
To wake you for school though
Your crack baby sister screams all night
Or your crack head parents plans and
Dreams don't come true for you
Cause there always missing in action...

When you can hold a would be baby glob
Of blood in the palm of your hand
Without shedding a tear...
And as if the STD didn't burn enough
You tell your man, you got *it*
He gave it to you, go to see the docta, man
For you get burnt again...
Thinking of the food and rent
Tuition funds and foodstamps already spent
But you can be a ghetto mack
Without a whimper take the nuked coffee
He spills upon your back....

When your Doctor, Doctor needs to get real
And decides after 10 years you don't fit the bill
He's moving up in life
He no longer needs a wife
At least not you, What can you do?
When love's untrue
Yet twice you bore his seed
And you got nada for your kids to eat
Listen like a child as he plays with your head
All the while there's another in his bed
Yet you believe him when he fixes his mouth to say
We'll be together again someday

So off you ship your only kids
Now all that you had is his...

When your face can be the canvas
For the black man's grief and rage
Yet you smile and stay versatile
Whenever you grace the stage
Cause the purest love today
Is rewarded for the gifts no man
Can take away....

These are but a few voices of Punany
Cast members of this natural life
Not preaching just teaching and sharing
Caring with hard reality and honesty
Even the Cherry Moon fades
When the sun takes her place
In the light you can see clearly
And make change

See Roni....
Punany is but a metaphor
The safer sex ... a cover
For the LTD's (Love's Transmitted Diseases)
Infecting our well being, our health
Latex signifies respect of others and self
Protection from those, who would make us their ho's
You know, the haters, business or otherwise
Who start shit in our lives and go

You say you won't stand for Punany
But will stand with Punany undisclosed
Untold on stages
While an intimate war rages
Between jaded hearts, longing pussies
And twisted dicks
Got the same heros who support you
Sick, yet smiling, confidently bullshitting
His public into thinking there's some cure

Besides self respect and love for the poor
Who can seldom afford, virtue

Sister, Sister I'm doing big things with backstreet dreams
That's you, Hollywood poet superstar
Donning Ebonics like its a lucrative fad
With big funds and love coming from
Deadly sports stars, creeping LA Thrillers
What do money don't prove?
Dead man walking
Dead woman laying
Dead people grinning
False hope giving
I got a million or two or four
And believe me, family value people
I ain't sick no more
Creep with me but
Don't bring your dirty deeds to my stage
Though indeed they stage true backstreet, backseat dramas
Who will stand for Punany?
Everyone will lay down for Punany
But who will free her soul?
Stone throwers, Merging Christian ideologies
Let the Backstreet virgin
Spit her diverstion from truth and
Cast the first stone
Here I stand; East Oakland Jezebel
Will tell them just how it T I S
Just how Punany bleeds
You will never silence me
The stones you throw
Will make holes in my soul
But believe blood will trail
Like soldiers through trenches
Streaming til they join the ranks of
Punany blood sisters in this battle field where
Sex and death face off in this war for life
Let the haters come, for victory will be won
Charging toward bullshit optimists
Two edged sword piercing names and social ID's

Of infected lovers from her mouth
Tattooed with bed sores ripe as a decomposing ass
In the Middle Eastern desert war path

Yea, victory ain't always a pretty thing
Death be fresh out of gospel hyms
To rock into your MIC
Jesus might can fix it, but some folk just ain't wit it
They say you got to believe it to receive it
Most folks just can't conceive it
From where they sit in backstreets
Dangling off a needle; on sheets of motels
trying to pay their monthly bills
Or just loosing themselves in the concrete hell
Where Jesus' footprints leave no trail
I say you got to receive it to believe it
So why fo' you wanna save the saved?
I come to preach about sin to the righteous
Open the blind Hollywood eye
So the righteous may get
Up off the high horse and walk the road Jesus'
Died for.... this lowly one,
The one you cross the street to avoid
Them high falutin' Christians
Donning Jesus like a ploy
A game to hide the shame of not being about
Your father's business

Where your roots be?
In money, the evil green, OK?
Go head girl be stuck up in LA,
True backstreets are fucked up
Cast your stones while I'm hung up
on the Punany Cross
Where is my thief?
Where is the gangbanger?
Where is the hype?
Give me the whore
Who bleeds my bloodtype

Ghetto Girl Blue

Never Less than a Man

What do you want to be?
The teacher asked the class
Dahlia awaited her turn in anticipation at first
    But when her turn to speak finally arrived
Having heard the boy's dreams and
the girl's dreams of being
dreamed of
by the boys

Dahlia froze.
St st st st stuttered...suddenly her tongue
began to swell in her mouth
she thought she would choke if she spoke of her dream
to grow up to
be a man
    She could not speak, They would not understand
    she was a pretty girl
    pretty wasn't hard to attain in
    a city plagued with long nights and bad nutrition
    she never gave pretty much thought
        But pretty helped her out a lot
The teacher stroked her cheek and patted her head
"It's OK Dahlia, pretty girls can afford to be shy"
    If she were a boy, refusing to cooperate
    that teacher would have given her a lashing with the
    big ruler she called her persuader
    it wasn't cruel and unusual punishment
    it was tough love, the teacher told the boys
    she was preparing them to face a cruel
    and usually punishing world
Dahlia stood up, walked to the front of the class
grabbed the persuader and gave it to the teacher
she gritted her teeth and bent forward
    Each lash propelled her into her freedom
    freedom from pretty
    after that day,
Dahlia didn't want to be a man,
she would be anything but
never less than a man.

Milk Man

Came home yesterday morning,
My man being gone
Done started a poetic psalm
That stick to my mind like
History stick to time

Paged my man yesterday morning
Took 13 minutes to call me back
Asked my man yesterday morning
Why he gone at am when the sky was still black
He went to get milk yesterday morning
My man answered without a stutter
There was milk in the refrigerator yesterday morning
"Oh, is there?" Said my man his eyes all a flutter
"Yes", I answered my man yesterday morning
Turning the cold glass bottle of milk to my lips
It left a mustache on my heated face
That maybe made me think I was a man
Yesterday morning
Don't know bout the body but
Milk can do the soul some good
When it's in a cold glass bottle
that was taken for granted
by a man who used it as an alibi once too often
once too many mornings
got his Momma mourning
over a closed casket 'cause
blood, and milk and glass can't clean up to good
when a body's been laying up with all that
drying in the sunlit day on my back porch
till the milk man found him

Every time these bars clink
I hear milk bottles shake
Mind thinking, soul singing

Milk Man, Milk Man,
His head has sprung a leak
Didn't remember I warned
Him about it, way last week
Milk Man, Milk Man
Your lies are broken down
When you come up with them
I want to beat you down

My body, you say I owe you
Respect you say is due
That's a little more love than I'll give you
Cause honey this woman ain't new

What?
You gone, find another woman
You ain't gon' pay PG & E
You gon' take my hair weave
And throw it in the street

Oh! You talking mighty whitey
Like you go some balls
Like you feeling tall
Make you feel real small
I dip them balls in alcohol

Keep on talkin' hear?
Bout turning off the heat
Shutting off the cable
So I can't see BET

See, Terry Mac's got me peepin
That you been out freaking
Knockin boots
And spendin loot
That's supposed pay for

Milk Man, Milk Man
Bet I can
Stop your mouth from running
Slice up your lying tongue and
Beat you in the head
Till you laying dead
When the

Milk Man Milk Man
Coming humming a song 'bout
Doing the body good

Patrol Sirens, Billy clubs

Ghetto Express
Just twenty five cents

Ghetto Girls Don't Lactate

I was born in the Ghetto
Addicted to the pipe
Once my mother was a woman
Now she's just a hype

Ghetto Girls don't lactate
They perpetrate
Motherhood
I wish I could
Find a rhyme
That speaks of positivity
Possibly
It's me
Probably
It be
The Ghetto
In me
Invincibly
Negative
Society wouldn't give
A black woman a chance
If she doesn't sing
And dance
And I doubt
I got
A got Damn Thang
To sing about
Can't dance without
Nutrition

Of my soul
Momma would hold
Me to nurse
On breasts so dry
She'd cry
So I
Could
Drink her tears
Try
To know why
My Momma was a ghetto girl
Addicted to the pipe
Once she was a woman
Now she's just a hype

Black babies
With souls that are thin, malnutrition
Become black men in the pen
Black women who are
Whores, high on gin
'Cause
Ghetto Girls don't lactate
They perpetrate
Motherhood

But before you
Point one finger at my mother
Point three back at yourself
And in her worn shoes
Walk a mile
For it takes a village to raise
One child
It takes a village
To raise one child

The Little Nigger Who Was

(In V Part Harmony)

PT. I
The Nigger Clone

Who is the Nigger the world in waiting for?
Is he light, bright
Damn near white
An educated multi-linguist
Content on the last rung
Of the corporate ladder
Where there he poses no threat
And to be nonthreatening is his single aspiration
Having no will, desire
plan or preparation to take
White money, White Hollywood, White blood
White woman
With a solitary stroke of the
Monstrous niggertude
Christianity bought
Civil Rights bartered and Affirmative action sold?

PT. II
The Nigger Wild

Who is the nigger the world longs to tame?
Does his fierce rhetoric
Still call from panther graves
For hot school lunches
And Chinese artillery
And socialist reform
And freedom from
Slavery of mind?

Is the American soil that consumes his fight
as sweet to his lips today as the day he realized
Niggers were American first
and bowed before the world to kiss it?
Could professional gigs
And popularity and novelist opportunity
And wine and women
And song and sonnet
And hop and the white lady
And the soul chilling prison bars and walls
That partition Black body stench
 reminding him of slave ships, tame him?

PT. III
The Nigger in the Glass Box

Who is the Nigger the World fears?
Is that his face on the six O'Clock
News hour after hour
Racking and stacking votes for politicians
Who listen to the populous cries for more chains,
More pigs, more judges, more law school scholarships
To keep shipping him away
More further away from the clean white people
In the clean white houses
Where clean white fear quivers and gazes
Upon black faces of the six O'clock news hour
Statistical charts
Measuring his blood draw and spillage
Securing bars of his concrete village
Until it is his own wish to blemish society's screen
His Black Power wish fist not raise but shackled
On the six O'Clock news hour?

PT. IV
The Lost Nigger Loved

Who is the Nigger the
World has set free?

Does he roam mindlessly through piss
Stained ghetto streets in quest for
Victims and guns
And knives and black freedom fighter
Tongues to slice
Is he in a Nigger's house
Answering to the name of brother, son
Cousin, uncle, daddy, lover?
Does the blood of his victims
Paint the foolish woman's walls
And nails, and straighten her hair in
Nigger salons and dress her back
And moisten her pussy
So his wrath don't burn so bad or
Cut so much or swell so soon
He'll leave to find another
Who will lick her battle scars cleaner
With each stroke of the foolish woman's
Tongue that spills lies of forgiveness
And pardons for trickery his story
That brought her murdering
Nigger lover to this?

PT. V
The Little Nigger Who Was

Fear not Oh world, Wait not and want not too
For the nigger you seek is already dead
And master's plantation
Done turned to shit
And master's woman
Writhes in heat on your
Bed of iniquities
Because all the Niggers are dead
And master's ways have taken root
Deep inside, causing transformations
That have not disguised
but have surely changed

the Nigger who used to be
Fear not, Oh world, Wait not and want not too
For the Nigger you seek, The Happy Clone,
The Angry Black Rhetorical Soldier
And the self-hating black one too
Are surely, undeniably
Already as dead as
any lynched Nigger in history
And all that is left
Is me

Sanctified & Satisfied

"How you gon' get good lovin'
From a man you keep breakin' down?"
"Oooh he may be tired
Black men they do get tired
And oh, his soul may be crying
Fighting the 400 year fight
When he's feeling weary
Give him that sexual healing
And he will always stay
Sanctified and satisfied
Strong and ready, to fight another day
And ooh he may be shame
Black men they do feel shame
Knowing she doesn't see him
The way she use to see him
And no, she don't do him
Like she use to do him
Wash him in your sugar rain
One thousand and one different ways
And his soul will reverb

Sanctified and satisfied
Strong and ready, to fight another day
He'll keep the food on the table
If you treat him like he's able
Girl you've got to
Whisper to his body
That you ain't lost the faith
With all the skill those lips can
Over and over again
''He'll never be anything less than a man''
And he will rise
Sanctified and Satisfied
Strong and ready to fight another day"
 "You got to hold him…
Can you mold him, hah..
Where he fit
In that shrine of forgiveness..
You got to treat him, hah
You betta be recognizin'
Or you'll be realizin'
An empty, lonely bed

Their Souls Have Eyes

There was a man who thought
He had it all
Never a cause had he
To stop and think
He was on borrowed time
Every sliver of gold
Every particle of diamond
Must be returned to the dust
His victims would fuss
And get on the bus
So the world might
Some day see
How greed and envy
Create poverty and misery
A human condition
So inhumane
It was hard to name
No fortune and fame for the few
Could ever rectify
The bodies that die
While the soul still pines
longing to be free
"Woe is me"
The victims screamed
Misery loves company
If you think he said,
"I won't go down without a fight"
You are sad in your misgivings
A slave for a thousand dark nights
Is a slave forever
If you think he said
"I'll go it alone"
So the evil one will know
Power is not just in numbers

But, in individuals
Sad words he uttered
As he died, trying to be hard
And behind prison bars
And in drive-by cars
And in drug raids
And with white girls
In the palisades
And at the victim of the
Wholly Hollywood
Talking gibberish
"It's all good"
"Don't worry be happy"
And "Just do it"
As he died American
A fist full of dollars stuffed
Down his dreams
While dying he uttered
Iniquities
The ancestors may never
Forgive
If you think he said
Something about mountain tops
And dreams
It seems your quite ambitious
See the abolitionists stopped short
Not revealing the true directive
And the slave is programmed to further
The plan alone when public scrutiny
Public policy and PC politics
Sucks the rich man's dick
Imagery of an America free
Of even the threat of black
How can one abolish slavery
Without abolishing the slave?
And even in his hour of honor
He is headed for his grave
"I won't go down, I won't go down
I won't go down
Without my brother"

Iniquities he uttered
The ancestors
May never forgive
Take this advice for as long as you live
Or until your brother pulls you down
Their souls have eyes and their watching
Everything you do
Even if it's true
That you do what you do
Because you've been
Programmed to

Simile

Pain be to Black people
what crack be to the hype
What the hype be to the dealer
what dealer be to guns
what the guns be to the government
what the government be to the poor
what the poor be to themselves
Revolution, Revolution, Revolution
for real, free will, for free will
Pain is as natural as pressing combs,
silk wraps, acrylic tips,
kitchen sink perms, no lye
won't burn unless you get it in your eye
The changes we make for appearance's sake
when the heart aches for
Revolution, Revolution, Revolution
for real, free will, for free will

Once More... for the First Time

My arms are spread as wide open as my heart
Waiting to embrace you
Come to me daddy
Complete me
Once more for the first time

The flame was just about out
It was 'round midnight
Be only a few mo' hours
'n that old cock 'd be crowing
Waking up that hunger only you can fill

Got my brain pining for you
Paining with thoughts of you
Though you are gone
'Cause I'm still waiting
Fo' science to make a shampoo
Strong enough to wash erotic memories
Of our bodies moving in time to nature's
Pulsating demands, out of my hair

Seem lately
My cupboard's empty
'Cept for a couple fragile glass jars
Full of memory seeds
Seeds don't taste so bad when you starvin'
Stand in the window hoping midnight pining
Will subside when God brings another day to me
While I wash down another memory
With my morning bluesin', boozin
Homicide shots
Suicide's not
What I had in mind this time

"Just trying to do a 187 on
Them thoughts of you
And me dancing carefree
Under a ghetto sun

Come to me daddy
Merge with me until we are so close
Together we are more like one
Than either of us are when we are alone
Come to me Daddy
Complete me
Once more for the first time
Sunrise comes a little slower
When hearts grow weary from age
From loss
From longing
And loneliness
My life is empty without
A completed soul
Could you merge with me?
Once more for the first time

Thought I saw a flame that glowed
As bright as you did once
Invitational dance,
Beckoning me
Like shards of rock guitar
Soulful strings that bind spirits
Beyond the physical
I'm thinking of that light now
While the cock prepares to crow
I fix my lips to say
It is over
It is over
It is over
I have found another fire
Felt its flame burning desire
Insatiably through me
I fix my lips to say
It is finished
Like Jesus

I wanted to give up the ghost
And return home
To the passion of the rock guitar
Soulful spirits that bind
Beyond the physical
But in your eyes I saw a glow
Licking up into the
Heavens of your mind
Tried to rap my brain around
The possibility
That the thirst for life
That made me yours
Would keep me forever
And was not dead
Nor in the vibrating guitar strings
Of another you
I fixed my lips to say
It is done
It was a lie
I wanted to repeat
Into the bosom of this rising
Old familiar sun
Over and over
Until the cock crowed
Once more for the first time

Somebody's Somebody

Yes I'm short, sassy, red boned
ghetto slanging, freaky dressin'
no phone call returning
freckled faced, shit talking, dick teasing
daughter of a nigger lover
and yes I'm a high yellow sometimes
prissy ass bitch too.
But I'm also
Somebody's Loving Momma
Somebody's Mourning Child
Somebody's Sharing Wife
Somebody's Loyal Friend
Somebody's Sole-Soul Mate
Somebody's Faithful Follower
Somebody's Satisfied Punany
Somebody's Honest...
Somebody's Happy...
Somebody's Sweetest, Special Somebody

Just Like You

Whore

in this House

There's a whore in this house
Is it you or I?

I slave to the pulsating rhythm of love
For a man twice my age in spirit
My first daddy

You slave to the almighty dollar
Grinding away time
And years to feed a hunger
To measure against the Jones'
See his pretty wife with no opinion
See his pretty car without a blemish
Like his stuff?

There's a whore in this house
Is it you or I?

I don't want to fuck
To get access to the ATM machine
Whose receipt bears only one name
Of our union
Don't want to whore to buy groceries
Cook, clean, do laundry conditionally
Don't want to whore so that
I can be true to my hustle
To write these words
Over and over again until someone
Shall find their value
Name it, and make me free....
There's a whore in this house
Will he every be happy?

Ever stop the grind to hear the birds sing
Or smell the flowers in the garden
He works to tend?
Will he ever love me enough to set me free
Can a whore ever really be set free?

Once a whore
Always a whore
They say, We'll see
I'm preparing for flight
From my first daddy
Like a child away from home
for the first time
Readying myself for life 101
But I will not be alone
as long as I have memories
Teaching me how to mother
How to belong
And how not to
Not live

I'm pulling the prick out of my ass today
Like a baby weaning from the breast
There will be times the anus throbs
Even leaks to be filled with

Your power of MAN
but...
Guilt doesn't live here anymore
I will no longer be a whore
for postage stamps,
A whore to mail my manuscripts,
A whore to buy the books that teach me,
A whore since poverty keeps me
From more formal schooling
Pretty soon now he can curb

His competition
With my other lover
I.B.M.

I, Believe in Me
P.C.
Please Commit
Trying to tell my life story
He's written all over it
But can't bear to think it's telling
Will drive me from him
Keep me down
Foot on my back
Leash around my neck
Keep fueling my gift
With discouragement
I recognize you after all
Though not as smooth as some
Though not as debonair
Oh, contrarily I say to thee
Release me, least I dub thee
Pimp above pimps
Playing on my poverty
Promising stability if I
Jump through the
Hoops of Hope
Or over the broom
Like a wanton slave bride
Social conditioning keeping her
Welcoming master
Welcoming master
Well come master
Lay a little more pimp drag on me
When the going gets tough I what?
No longer shall
A pimp named guilt
Run me around the track
In my living room

There's a whore in this house
There's a whore in the house
There's a whore in this house
She's moving out

Sister's Wake Up Call

Let us pick up where Spike left off and
Wake Up —
Wake up sisters
The Brothers' spirits died long ago
Before ships ever reached an African port
When our purpose was to
Breed for field hands
To tend the soil
But now the brother's have no land to tend
Wake up Sisters
Let's pick up where Spike left off and Wake Up
Don't breed a child, raise a child
Don't breed a child, Raise a child
Don't Breed
A child, raise a child
For their futures lay as unmolded clay in the palm
of your freshly manicured hands
Walk past the Mac counter
Which calls to you to make up
To look like the calendar, poster video bombshells
Dropping into the Black man's lust
Insatiable lust to feed his deflated self image
When you are at the mall
Looking for something tight
Slinky and haunting to make lasting impressions
On a potential sperm donor
Think of these words
Wake up sister, don't breed a child
Raise a child
You get no points for doing what is necessary
should be natural to feed
What is yours
If you can not feed it, do not breed it

If you can not teach it
You don't need it
So I beg of thee
Pass by the new shoes and gold earrings
Sparkling from behind
Consumer glass
And buy a book for your child
Read to your child
And forego the $300 weaves
To send your child to a school unriddled with
Pushers and gamblers and would be role models
Stop talking about how the Black man
Is a dying breed and those who are alive?
Aren't fit for shit
Hell, lets be real
Can we really remember a time when Black men
 were fit to be called anything but shit
Dancing and shucking a jiving and spitting bullshit
Rhetoric behind Whitey's Back
Till Whitey offered government jobs
Threatened their freedom to be heard at all
And now like then
You are still alone
Except for the nights he comes to plant his seed
So that you may breed…..Don't
And if you must fulfill some need to bear a seed
Know that the seed and its vine
And the bloom is yours alone to tend
Don't talk about how the man ain't paying child support
When you never asked him if he wanted a child in the first place

And don't get mad at me
I feel your pain
Been in a your place
Felt love lies embrace my jaded, wounded, alone spirit
Calling
Doctor Feel Good to fix it
There are some things that I want
Selfish things that I need

To be completely human
But to be completely woman must be my mission now
I have my own child
But my man is on his way out
And I'll bet you one thing
You won't find my ass in the welfare line
One in the stroller
Two on the hip
Cause sex is mighty fine
But raising babies takes money and time
And honey
I done been fixed

Black Words Soft Spoken

When did black become a four letter word?
To me it looks like five
Who took the pride out of the
Jimmy JJ Walker jive
That kept our hearts light
In spite gun fights
Welfare oversights
Dog food dinners?
And who called Cosby a winner?
Except the few who could relate
No matter,
The pockets that get fatter
Ain't hanging off of baggy hip-hop rags
Or stretched across
Uncle Clarence Thomas' Ass
Just one big happy family of
Dancing nigger clones
Paper pushing drones
Pig skin thrown
Across a football field
Fist that wield
Fury into other black faces
While other races sit in
Ring side seats and
Watch another
Brother go down
Spear chuck another basketball
From tribes men so tall
Yet stand so small in their eyes
It's not a fight but a struggle
Fumble, scramble, tackle
So they can get another cluck cluck
Fancy dancing chicken coop fantasy
Make big Black Bucks

Make them a dollar
Yet Giggaboo Giggaboo quick to holla
I got it going on
Pennies in his pocket
Make him feel fine
Capitalistic vibe
Making him a star
But he won't get too far
Unless he sticks with his tribe
Can't we all just get along?
Black words
And soul verbs
Must be spoken softly
For they are listening
When you cry aloud
Black words soft spoken

Glass ceiling's got minds reeling
Got the suit some cash
Even boast some white ass
Corporate buck just stuck
On the lower rung of the ladder
Shuffles and yassirs piled high
On the platter he hoists
Above his head yet he kneels to serve
But got the nerve
To hate on young cats
That won't fake the funk
Willing to kill for the buck
Neither realizing they are
really the victims
Of systematic homicide
Genocide, suicide, confide the oneness
Of this so you can see
But don't speak of it too loudly
And if you tell them that I told you
I may meet my maker in a
Freak accident
Speakers speak, MLK say
A man not willing to die for something

Ain't fit to live
Matter's it, Man who lost your virtue
In the biblical tales of your
Abernathy brother...
What your willing to die for?

Black words
And soul verbs
Must be spoken softly
For they are listening
When you cry aloud
Black words soft spoken

This ain't fiction but fact
Ask Michael Jackson
Thought he was planning
To raise the roof off the mother
Store his Chocolate Milk
With the nondairy koshers
Don't give a fuck about the
Homosexual boy trying to come up
But Mike took their King's daughter
And fucked her
Got him quaking in the European dark
Waiting for his career to wake
And we didn't get his back
Because it... Had no tribal marks
Airing dirty laundry
Will find them pondering
When to make their next move
Who to kill too soon
Rest in peace Tupac
Got clocked before
His destiny was ever fulfilled
Killed to join the ranks of black men
of different tribes
Whose causes weren't always
Embraced by all
No reason to eradicate their accomplishments
Just because their subliminal hints

Of revolution in all its shades of flavors
Don't agree with yours
You don't have to agree but try to see
That they are watching where
To make their next move
What to do with the press
What color to paint the news
How to infiltrate our blues
And fill another tomb
With black
Black Black
Believe Love And Collect Killed
Blackness
Anything black
Beautiful Black
Dignified Black
Hated Black
Disrespected Black
Embarrassing Black
Disenchanted Black
Anything Everything Black
Lest we all fall
For Black is the presence of all
But Sssshhh, don't tell them that I told you....
They are listening to Black words soft spoken

Shackles Don't Stop the Flow

You know I got it on my mind
Not sometimes, but all the time
Wanna spread my heart strings as wide
As Black can push them
Purse my lips and lose them
 In a deep throat Black Love Kiss
Want some of that Black Love
I never had, but nevertheless, I miss
Want it so bad I feel like a ho'
Wanna work it out all over the ghetto track
Get me a Black Love pimp
So we can win the ghetto back
Wanna fill my 40 ounce bottle
With some hot malt Black Love juice
Pour libations till pains erased and
Our shackles...they get a lil' loose
>Black love is always coming
>Bars can't damn the flow
>Black love is always coming
>No powder house can shut her down
>She don't need to partner up
>She'll come alone if she must

GGB

Ain't scared of an institution
For, Black love is the Revolution
Silently unsuspected, creeping like a thief in the night
Twisted, angry, bitter, hard, raw, uncontrollably real
Answering to bitch, nigger, whore, sucker.... &
"Damn, I love you, you sorry ass Black mothafucka!"
...Unrelentlessly resourceful, while plans of escape are abrew
Grinning, shuffling, jiving, and "Oh, Missa Massa, Lordy, what we gon' do?"
Answering to Blackie, Darkie, Mammy, Nigger,, Giggaboo
Die a million deaths and live two million mo'
Baptising whitey in blackened blood... before we go
You know? Black love is always coming,...
Even shackles can't stop the flow

No Such Thing

What happens to a
"dream deferred"?
Nothing
For no such a thing exists
There are no dreams
Only memories of things past
And visions of things to come
There is no such thing as
" dreams deferred"
Only failure to learn from history
And inability to plan ahead
There is no such thing as failure
Only those who never try
There is no such thing as winning
Because learning never ends
There are only those who set goals
Reach them
And quit

My Brother's Keeper

Who does that
High Yellow, Octoroon, Quadroon
Piss-Colored, Mixed Bred, Mulatto, Wanna-be-White,
Black Honky
Think she is anyway?

Colorless Spirit painted on Black Soul
Too busy spreading love and thinking of
My beautiful son, and the challenge before me
To give him a life, better than my own;
A life that doesn't teach him, his enemy is not
In the White House, the Pentagon, the County AFDC
Office
The Court House, The Oakland Hills, or even in the
cheesing half-smile
Of the Asian immigrant store owner selling
Two dollar toilet paper around the corner:
But in the hateful words of his Brother
My brother's keeper
Is there such a creature
And is he black?

Junkie Heaven

In ghetto streets
Where freedom junkies creep
In quest of their much needed rest

Poverty
Boggles the
Mind
Militia never rests

Revolution in the hood
An institution
Not understood

Mercenaries
Of the underworld
Unfurl death
In tiny doses

Through smoke and hits
And crack head fits
That permeates the brain

Poverty has no shame
No rules to the game
Can't remember your name

If you never knew it
When inadequacy fuels it
No bed to rest your head

No daddy to tuck you in it
No motherland for a slave
No Christian marker on your grave

Just want to fly
To deeper depths
Where pain is a fantasy
Like the one Whitey
Whispers from a couch
One hundred dollars an hour
Yours boils, hands toil
Sweat drips, smoke releases power

Live tiny little death minutes
When it's easier to fly
Some place In the sky
Beyond task's wondering eye
Is Victory
Standing at the gate
At the end of the road
Most traveled through history

Your soul tis of He
He will welcome you home
To a land you've earned
The right to call your own

Antirevolutionaryexcuseism

Don't you call me no nigga
And neveryoumind that I ain't got no job
Can't feed my kids, never leave the hood
High times are good,
Thought I should, never would... Marry a Black Woman
Money squanderin, club wanderin', forever hollerin'
just quite bother'n me
And don't you call me no nigga
I'm a King without a throne
Can't make it on my own,
some people
wanna keep a brotha' down
So just leave me be, to be infantile
juvenile, stuck on trial by
The White Man
Alright, there I said it God dammit
They need to confess it
Like Uhuru, regret it
30 acres and a mule?
When I'm gon' get it
I want respect shit
Could I just get my GA check?
Until I gets Rest & Tutions
Whitey gon' pay... GA all gottdamn day!!
Maybe feel my stripes
Even pay wit' his life
But for now, I'll just take his fine white wife.

Niggah They Call You

Niggah they call you and
Niggah you call yourself
And wonder why nobody treats you like a man
If you could understand
And see what I see
Niggah you wouldn't act like and
Niggah you would not be
But you're too high to see
I'm looking for a king to get high righteously
Between my loving arms
With a strong Black family
No king could cheat, steal and lie
Disrespect his woman, himself and his tribe
To elevate himself to a crack Hades high
The Devil has known your body
Bought and paid for your soul
Still don't know your name
    Yet he's calling you
      Niggah.....Niggah.....Niggah
Meet me in this Hades high
Forget your family and your tribe
Forget your missing crown
     Get up get down get funky get hiiiiigh
     Niggah!
No black man would ever answer
For no black man could ever hear
     The Devil's calling you, calling you Niggah
     Calling you Niggah
Want's your soul
   Singing I got five on it
     Don't you want it? Niggah!
You are his ho and he fucking you good...
Like a real pimp should
Sucking, consuming your African seeds and your health
Got you creeping with stealth
Quick to relieve a brother of wealth
Ho chose his pimp, still he don't know your name
Take another hit niggah, introduce yourself!!!

White Massa Fa Toby

What's your name boy?   *Toby*
What's Your name boy?   *Toby*

Toby don't be gettin high
Toby don't be gettin high
Toby don't be gettin high

Who was that, ran 'n' catch ole Kunta?
Took 'im to his foot chopping day
Say old Kinte jis a fool
          fo' eva havin' run away.....

If your side of town was a plantation...
Yea, Who would rule the city nation?
Who would be the slave...
And who would dig the graves?
Whose bodies would be buried there?
Who be the rebel or dream to dare?
Whose babies would be alone?
And for his sins, whose master would atone?
What face has he? Who be his kin?
What shade and color be his skin?
What control has he?
Who plants his seeds?
Bears his fruit controls his fields?
Who pull da trigger of da gun he wields?

Bet your dealer   is the Devil
Wanna kill you   just a little
Talkin 'bout get hiiiiiiiiiiigh   niggah wit me....
Get hiiiiiigh niggah wit me!

Slipping through the biways sideways
Jus trying to make a dollar
Never hear their babies cry, never hear them holler!

Toby don't be gettin high
Toby don't be gettin high
Toby don't be gettin high

Bet your dealer   is the Devil
Wanna kill you   just a little
Talkin 'bout get hiiiiiiiiiiigh   niggah wit me....
Get hiiiiiigh niggah wit me!

What you gon do when there's no one left to blame
An if old master take his back
Just what in hell would be your name?!!!

Would You, Could You, In a Boat?

Would you walk through fire for me?
Would you drink my bath water?
Would you cry all night till I came home?
Would you spend you last dime on the promise of my time?
Would you forsake your father and your mother just to be my lover?
If I died would you never touch another?
Would you change careers to calm my fears?
Would you kill for me?
Rob and steal for me?
Weep when I cry?
Ache when I hurt?
If I cut myself would you bleed?
Fuck until you drop just to meet my needs?
Would you? Could you?
      Stand out in the rain just to catch a glimpse through my window pane?
Would you, could you change your name?
Would you love me if there was no sex?
Would you want me if I was fat or if I had no hair,
      Embarrassed you with the clothes I wear?
What if I was horribly disfigured, walked with a limp or was

smitten by a pimp?
What if I was on drugs, never gave you kisses and hugs?
> Would you still be in love?

What if I didn't work just vegged out on TV?
Would you be glad just to be around me?
What if I spent my whole paycheck on my personal needs?
Never seemed to talk to you except when I was in need?
> Crept around at night doing dirty deeds?

Would you? Could you? In a boat
> Expose your vein and shoot my bullshit like dope?

What if I beat you? Threatened to leave you?
Called you names and put you down whenever my friends were around?
What if I got you pregnant but was hesitant to make this thing legitimate?
What if I was your wife but never wore your ring?
For my love would you do most anything?

NO?

I wouldn't do that shit for you either!

Little Mary's Hippie Song

Hey Little Mary there's penance to be paid
Hey Little Mary there's penance to be paid

Hey Little Mary you're digging a deep grave
Hey Little Mary you're digging a deep grave

He don't love you, just wants to
Run up in your soul
Steal your body's treasures
Leave an empty hole

Can't make a whore a housewife
Can't make a crook go straight
Can't live truth and a lie too
Your death wish has sealed your fate!!!

Hey Little Mary there's penance to be paid
Hey Little Mary there's penance to be paid

Hey Little Mary you're digging a deep grave
Hey Little Mary you're digging a deep grave

He don't love you, just wants to
Run up in your soul
Steal your body's treasures
Leave an empty hole

You've got a mighty big
        A mighty big
                A mighty big
Cross upon your back

A mighty steep
        A mighty steep
                A mighty steep
Hill to track
Ask sweet Jesus bet he'll tell you
                     It don't give no slack!!!!!

Hey Little Mary there's penance to be paid
Hey Little May, Hey Little Mary, Hey Little Mary,
HEY!......................................ASHAY

Alibi African

Alibi are magicians
Who perform illusions on the mind
Alibi are fate
That has yet to be written
Alibi are scholars
Who think little of natural wisdom
Alibi are liberals
Who try to save us from ourselves
Alibi are impartial
Loyal to no one cause
Alibi are heroes
Who keep pride in our hearts
Alibi are tricksters
who make pride and excuse the same
Alibi are most adept
at making scapegoats of the next man
Alibi live in all of us
Much the same as truth
Changing like a chameleon with the times
Yet beneath alibi and truth,
Who screw like crack lovers on
The piss stained box springs
Of the African Mind
Lay Doubt
A promising third member
To the incomplete trinity
Of the Alibi African

The brother with dreads in his hair
Hides his despair
In white women who do not share
The history of his impotent manhood

Alibi tells him not to fret
God has not made a black woman yet
Who could shut up Long enough
To bow to his missing crown
Unless he slaps her down

The sister gives herself body and soul
For the price of silver and gold
Exchange to any man who can afford
Her freedom chains
Alibi tells her she is not a ho
Just a single mother with children who grow
Fast and need school clothes

The hustler who believes
He only used to be a slave
Bucking and shuffling and hustling
The whites man's guns and drugs
To keep him free from corporate entity
Much like Black Slave owners
Alibi tells him if he does not supply
To troubled minds that need to fly
Somebody else surely will

Black People who keep changing their names
Like hairstyles, curls to perms to braids
Though the texture underneath remains the same
African American, colored, mixed, mulatto, Nubian,
Cape Verdian, Creole and New Yorican Soul
Labels that make us less that a whole
Till Black isn't simply
Black
Alibi tells them it is the
Exercise of the one freedom
The white man can not take away

Those who believe African
And righteousness are synonymous terms
Though absent and anonymous
Our righteous brothers remained
Never donning a gun or setting sail
Or giving us a righteous name
Alibi tells us there are opposites
In every natural thing
Therefore if Whitey is a Devil facade
The Black Man must be God

For those who dare to listen
And contemplate their doubt
They'd learn that Africans are merely men
Who introduced a system
To a man he couldn't check
And that if White men were truly scared of us
He wouldn't have his foot on our necks

Doubt will tell you not the truth
You don't want to hear,
but the hard reality you fear
That a slave is never a free man
Just an ex-slave with slave mentality

And to change a name can't change a mind
The sad fact that Black is always Black
An African American
Pimp, pusher, whore, hustler
Even the third eye motherfucker
Must get the next ones back
And remember from whence we come
For every one of us remains
A Nigger in America

A Song for Old Souls

You used to call me your boo
Now you say we're through
O' Lord
What can I do?
My man
Just ain't been true
Said you'd love me forever
Plus a day or two
Guess it's the twelfth of never
'Cause Lord
My man and me ain't together
You used to call me your boo
Now you say were through
O' Lord
What can I do?
My man
Just ain't been true
No man could do me
Quite the way you do, see
You make grey skies blue
Make my body cry for you
My heart don't bust a beat
Unless you bust a move
It ain't only me baby
Even my kids love you
You said you'd love me forever
Plus a day or two
Guess it's the twelfth of never
'Cause Lord
My man and me ain't together
I just sitting alone singing
A song for old souls
Marking my calendar
For the twelfth of never
'Cause Lord, my man and me ain't together

The Devil's Mass

It's no different
Tell me sister, how could I judge you
We are the same
Me and you
Given to this depth of love
which is more difficult
to understand than
the scientific theories that brought us here,
To this, man's world
We wait patiently for
reciprocation
accepting shallow demonstrations of...
And twisted interpretations of...

Love

What is it after all?

...Monday night football
games that shame me while
I lay on the floor
Beneath his feet
Shaking at his threats to dare me to speak

...The rhythm of our fights
rocking my babies to sleep
...The lash of his belt
Then the sudden gentle change, so strange
When he kisses my welts
Speaking softly into my chapel
With confessions of his sins
Spitting his burdens at the throne ... Of my love
And I, so desperate and passionate
Seeking the kind of love that's hard to get

From anyone save self ... Accept it
Speaking through the pained window of my soul
If you love me, confess it

Even when you can only express it
Through clinched fists, Venom lips
Violent, unquestioning thrusts of your hips
Breaking the glass, spanking that ass
Housewife whore in a pimp's class

In the Devils Mass ...
We worship

Hit me again papi
To let me know its true
Love just ain't love unless I am blue
Love just ain't love unless I am blue

The Mythology of A Black Man

Him cuss
Him scream
Him shout and fuss
Him wheel an' deal
Him steal an' kill
Him fo' the thrill
Him go to jail
Him bound fo' hell
Him lie
Him die
Him nev' try
Him don't care why
Him high on weed
Him plant him seed
Him woman in need
Him kids don't feed
Him run and hide

All because
Him cry inside

A Dick Witted Cop
&
His Wife

A man who findeth a wife, findeth a good thing
So the bible says
But your not a religious man
Guess I can't expect you to wear my wedding ring

If you were I'd say in a spiritual way
That you should appreciate the many parts I play
In this off Broadway production of love

Mother to your child
Friend when yours forsake you
Lover even when I'm tired
Trophy piece seldom admired
Chef to your finicky appetite
Keep my voice respectful and low
        even when we fight
I watched you promise under Jesus stars' and God's heaven
To love me until death do we apart
Every time you leave me here I don your wedding ring
Sit and think of death and impure things
It breaks my fucking heart
Excuse me if you lose me
To my profane rage

But I'm trying with human mind to understand some things
Custodian of lost souls of the Ghetto streets
Knowing all too well the Jezebels
That grind the track of your beat

When asked if you will don my ring today
It might get stuck on a fence you say
Or get lost when chasing hoodlums through an alley way
I try to think of my vows and wonder how
We will make it through another day
And try not to speak the evil things I think
Of where my wedding ring could really end up
But I'm no fool; Don't need cop school
To know a ring just salts your game
Somebody had better put out an APB
That dick witted cop is 'bout to lose me
'Cause truth be told
My ring might get lost in some street hustler's pussy

Jane Therese

My mother was a white woman
But a woman, all the same
For years I never thought much
Of white women
In fact, I didn't think of them much
In my mind's eye she was nothing
A dusty trophy piece
Never savoring the
bitter flavorings of grief
Placed on a Victorian mantle
Atop a fireplace seldom used
Silently worshipped
From Big House - To old slave shack
Never knowing abuse
The suffering of blacks
And so went my Negro Creed
Anything unpained has got no need
To be freed
My mother was a white woman
But a woman, all the same
When I was a little black girl
Ghetto Orthodox
Pumping through my veins
She would wait
Gift in hand and smile stretching
Across the milky skin of her face
As animated as my unease
The fear of kids seeing us
Invaded my senses leaving no place
For love, a touch, a kiss,
A mother-daughter's embrace
On this her once a week visiting day
Would have confirmed the truth
... of the Devil in my blood
But to her I was nothing less

Than her sweet black baby girl
The jewel of her emerald eye
A manifested promise of a time
Passion was as sweet
as the wine she drank
To numb her...
Old history when my missing father
So tall, so fine, so rich in soul, so black
Kissed her gently and
Darlingly loved her back

My mother was a white woman
But a woman, all the same

I hardly cared or noticed
The men who steadily came
To beat her down and kill her slowly
To ease their wretched shame
Too weak to fight, to ashamed to let me stay
She packed up her black baby
And sent me safely away
I never saw the pedestal, you see
Crumble beneath her calloused feet
Never heard the taboo drums
Resounding through the hopeless song
She played for each black man she'd meet
Buffalo soldier, I am the land of America
Rest your weary feet
They answered her call
One after the next
Each bigger, blacker, angrier
Than the one before
They spoke in an ancient tongue
She tried to interpret with her body
Giving her very best
But still they needed more
Pain grown bitter with time
Spilled like the wine she drank
To numb her
In a flurry of fists

Until there was nothing left

My mother was a white woman
But a woman all the same

How the pain does grow
When death is slow
The sunlight's glow simmering
Her uncloaked body's vapors
Crimson trailing like the dead
End roads she had taken
From all her open places
Maimed, Three days
Abandoned
And unclaimed
Now that I'm ready
To love her
Accept her, and proudly
Wear her name
Where is my Momma?
Where is Jane Therese?
Dead standing
In an unmarked grave

A King, See?

To marry a woman is to marry a home
I've got to be free to roam
Ghetto life is like the jungle
I'm as wild as the lion
Just got to be free
Cause like that beast
I'm a king too, see?
My territory is here
In the dark night of the city
My woman tribe; the scanks of Oakland
My wisdom robs them of hope then
Turns them out to pimps and
pushers who dope them
Till Daddy Sam saves them
When my children are hungry
The government can't raise them
I could reign for a year or two
'Til another King mashes through
I am as wild as the lion
Caged in my land by the sea
I've got to be free to be
The beast that rages inside of me
Just like that lion
A king too, see
A king too, see?

My Sister,
Sugar Water & the Ghetto Blues

Ghetto Girl Blue come spill that rhyme
Tellin' sweet stories of Ghetto
good times...Ain't we lucky we got 'em
They say the ghetto ain't a place
It's a state of mind
but I can't agree, see?
I know what it's like to go hungry
When ain't nothin to eat but poverty
Remember those days
When the rent wasn't paid
We were always two steps ahead of the landlord
'Cause honor was something we couldn't afford
When cash was obscure
But love was pure
Cause family was all that we had
Simple things made us glad
Like looking in the mirror and playing Bloody Mary
And sleeping in my sister's bed when the games got too scary
My sister's pillow smelled like spit, nature's iodine
    She'd hold my hand so that I could sleep
    And in the morning she'd change the sheets
    And we never told a soul
    About how nature helped us cope
    With the Ghetto blues that played in our hearts
    I thought even Ghetto Blues
    Couldn't tear me and my sister apart
    We didn't have money but we had big plans
    On Saturdays we'd make up a dance
    And talk about making it to Soul Train

>   Simple things are so sublime
>   While she nursed on the security of her thumb
>   I was haunted by the vision of a robber with a gun
>   And my fear made me want to pee
>   I knew if I got out of the bed
>   That robber was going to get me
>   And as the heat of my fear
>   Burned her leg and my crying burned her ear,

Or maybe becoming dancers for MJ
Oh we could dream all day
When we were tired
We'd give one another a glance
Smile and simply say, Hey Kool Aid !!!
But he didn't have time
Too busy making commercial's I guess
My sister said Sugar Water will do just fine
She'd mix two big glasses and we'd drink
Till we both were much too full to dance
And we'd suck on Now & Later's
We bought with pennies we found
And find a place on the floor where we could lay down
While I read her the stories I wrote in Ms. Tyler's class
And we would pass the time of day
Until the moon was cast
As we grew up into our teens
Our dancing days were distant dreams
'Cause we knew soon the welfare lady
Would set us free
To independently,

Fight poverty
My sister said she wondered if God had a plan
To fill her empty feelings with the love of a man
I set my sights for college and when I went away
She found a man who would lay her body on the bed
Raise his belt while he said
Ghetto girls lack discipline
Don't be back talking him
He'd kill her if she thought of walking
Her striped body then raped
Her mouth agape, though silence was all that could pass
Now before I visit her I write a story and fill a glass
With sugar water and put a pack
Of Now & Later's in my bag
I walk up through a maze and find her place
I offer her the Sugar Water
And read sweet stories of Ghetto Better Days
And imagine her eating the Now & Later's
While I lay atop her grave

Mostly Jane

Mostly Jane was a woman
Who found peace in no man
And mostly Jane was a thinker
Who wondered who's got her back?
And why black meant the blues
Sometimes she'd listen to Billy
Croon familiar tunes
That kept her misery in sync
With the rise and fall
Of each broken heart song
Sometimes she'd just sit back and think
Of daddies slipping tongues and pricks
To little girls who made them tricks
Of how words like foster and family and mother
Could be spoken in the same phrase
Sometimes she wished for better days
When memories weren't nightmares
She'd rock herself and hold her crying soul
And wish for a man who cares
All the while inside
Where her gloom resides
Her body readied itself for it's doom
Cause the walls of her room
Were becoming her tomb
As she tried all the while not to think
Cause most of all
Sweet Jane
Would drink

Brandy: Me & You

I love my Man
It just ain't true to say I don't
I need my man
Like a child need a breast
Like a working man need to rest
Like a bee need the flower
Like the clock need the hour
Like the river need the rain
to keep a-go with the flow
of natural thangs
Can't have you every day
Best believe he takes your place
But can't never fill your shoes
I love my man, It's true
Jis like the sinner shun Proverb
I'd leave him alone, lonely
Even black and blue
If he dare to find the nerve
t'come 'tween me and you
Straight up, not shaken or stirred
Brandy it's me and you

Small Feats

My Son,
I wish I could live my life twice...

The first to simply bathe in the essence of your glow
Like a ghetto child who has only known concrete fields
Running my blackening toes through
hot sands of motherhood for the first time,
The burning lashes of the sun whip across my flesh
Leaving lasting memories
of a place poverty may never let me be again

In the next life, I will teach you all of the things
I have learned from you in the first
Fearlessness, Unconditional Happiness
The love no man could ever rip from my body

Thump... Thump, I hear you knocking
on this fleshy door to the world
I will open a world greater than the one I left behind
Clean, Positive, Unscathed by
Fear, Death, Grief, The Hunger ... I have known
My humility no longer lay in
Flashbacks of ghetto days
When small feats kept us alive
My honor no longer in inner-city measures of

respect and pride or whether or not I could survive
another Spam dinner...
If I can make you glad to share this world with me
I am a winner of this race
"Freedom vs. The Chains of Fear"
You are but one dream fulfilled
Yet the greatest achievement of all
My body aches to set you free
My heart cries to keep you always with me
I have only my love to give you,
Take it all   Use it wisely
Never forget...
Somebody loves you
If only I knew that, before I knew you...

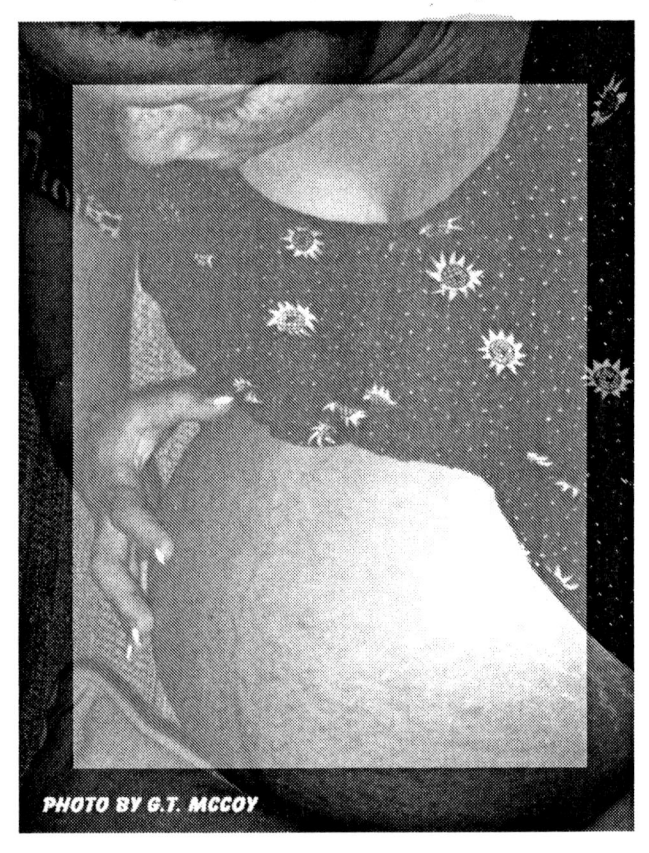

PHOTO BY G.T. MCCOY

Copy Cat Black

Copy cat, Copy cat
Where is your backbone?
White man's systems'
Got no, African rhythm
That's why you can't catch the beat
It's like that standardized test
You keep fighting to change
Kind of strange don't you think?
No matter our feat
We still call the ghetto our home....

Say Black, Why you biting that
Pale face, Ofay, Caucazoid, Whitey...
Could it be, you want something he's got?
I'm going to tell you a secret
He doesn't mind if I leak it
Cause he figures a genius you're not
While you obsessing over all his blessings
He going about his merry way
Planning for the day he can get his 10 percent
Up off this planet he done ruined
Awe ..
I tell you the only time he thinks about me and mine
Is to cast some fear around election time
Survival is his master plan
Got to keep the black man
From tainting the skin of his select 10

But that's not the secret; you all know that
Listen carefully now to what I'm trying to tell you Black
You got to stop half-assing or you'll catch hell's sorrow
If you're going to dance with the devil
in the pail moonlight
You gotta know the sun will be up tomorrow

Copy Cat, Copy Cat
Check out the scene
Poverty, envy, jealousy, the love of money
Done turned you from black to green
It's the Jedi mind trick in full effect
Your head hurts so I'm a chop you in the neck
You better stop your belly aching and look around
Black man get a plan 'cause its going down
Now you may get angry 'bout what I'm gonna say
But the ships for outer space, are fueling up, bound for some
no Black Man place
And just whatcho Black behind
gon' do without the white man anyway

Now that I've gotten your attention
I'd like to mention a few items that
Keep us confused, because without government jobs,
Prisons, welfare, Hollywood and German cars
It might be kind of hard
to live the lives we've come to lead

Oh, I say to you today you don't have to love
One another just love yourselves truly,
and every one of us can succeed
At conquering our demon and
I don't mean Whitey
I'm talking 'bout that green sucker called **GREED**

Bare wit me now because Miss Punany feels like having
church this evening....
Awe! Don't get me wrong, ain't nothin' wrong with wanting
things
But you got to be willing to work for the things you want:

We want a job but we don't want to work...
We want to have friends
but we don't want to be a friend to others
We want to be served but we don't want to serve others
We want to be kept but we don't want to keep others
We want to be helped but we don't want to help anybody

We want to be loved but we don't want to love others
We want respect but we don't want to give it
Want to call ourselves NIGGAHS
but can't nobody else call us that
We want a recording contract
but we don't want to go on tour
We want to be rappers without kicking knowledge
We want to be musicians and can't play an instrument
We want education without going to college
We want attitude without aptitude
We want solitude in company
We want unity without community
We want pleasure without pleasing
We want foreplay without teasing
We want sex without foreplay
We want family without marriage
We want a home without responsibility
We want children without pain
We want to be mothers without mothering
We want lovin'... Without loving
Brother's want babies but they can't afford them
We want Black businesses but we don't support them
We want to keep up with the Jone's
but we don't even know them
Ladies want to be paid for sex but they ain't in prostitution
We want conflict without resolution
We want restitution and can't even spell it
We want forty acres and can't even harness a mule
We want to go back to Africa
and don't even have ferry toll
We want a Black President and don't even go to the polls
We want to be African-American without being American
We want to stop the violence without turning in our guns
We want civilization without being civil
We want to murder but we ain't ready to die
We want power without honor
We want pleasure without pain
We want demonstrations without altercations
We want freedom without independence
I'll say it again Welfare Recipients...

We want freedom without independence
We want hope without belief
We want to call ourselves Muslim
...Never stepped foot in a Mosque
We want to call ourselves Christian
Going to church on Easter Sunday
We want Buda without self-reflection
We want peace without surrender
We want Christianity without Christ
We want joy without Jesus
We want Glory without God!

Copy Cat! Copy Cat!
Get a plan

Hypothesis Now

If White is as opposite Black as
Satan is opposite God...
and:
If the white man is the Devil then
the Black man is God?

Gabriel betta put down the trumpet
crank up the ghetto blasta
dip the chariot in candy apple red
drain the River Jordan
fill it withmalt liquor
unharness the white horse
saddle the scapegoat
bag up some rap lyrics
and mark the pearly gates with a
"Drug Free Zone" sign...
Get Mary Magdeline some
Daisy dukes and a release form
cause there's a heaven for a gansta
He's making videos
for the Armagaedon hos
but he fussing bout his 16 percent
while supping at the
last soul food supper
a meeting of divine minds
omnipotent yet can't figure out
shit but the split of the cash advance...
Guess who's coming to dinner?

My Blackened Heart

A Letter to Myself.......

I was reading in a book one day... It seems like only yesterday but it was a few years back... About a woman who was a ho for sometime yet seemed surprised to find this fact to be true. I pondered the possibility of whoring myself, or worse, allowing someone to pimp me out without my knowing, without my permission. I could never take money from strangers for sexual services and give the cash to a brother as I sit obliviously in a brothel, full of sisters like me, to the fact that men were using us.

As I read the books to follow the author's autobiographical series I saw the metamorphosis of her life and self image. How she took each experience and learned from it living often barely surviving each day and filling them with hope for tomorrow.

In recent times I have evaluated my own life examining it for signs of pimps and of the knowledge they kick so well ... it can manifest itself as self fulfilling prophecy.

I've decided to rid my life of people who would use my tarnished history and lace their game by using me, this body, this mind, this soul, and all the love my blackened heart has managed to preserve.

So I bid farewell to an old school pimp who claims to be my soul mate and in doing so to old history we made together that may have changed me forever.

Fare well to ho tactics and pimp practice and hello to a future full of hope and promise.

You feel me?

Peace... (Not as in I'm out, but as in may you enjoy rest in love)

Dear Diary,

Wednesday October 17th, 2001 ... I celebrated my sophomore international television debut on BET. I rushed home from rehearsal for a play that would be performed live for film the following day. I dropped my bags as I came into the door, fumbled with the remote control to my manager's fancy digital cable. And although I could barely wait to see the Life Tracks presentation of The Punany Poets, I detoured on my way to the bedroom television set, to pour myself some champagne. I don't even drink champagne. But it didn't matter. It was what was in the house so I had to drink it. I had to drink anything, if and when there was anything to drink.

Dear Diary,

Thursday, October 18th, 2001

Everybody who was important to the success of the newest ventures for The Punany Project, including a film, books and CD's, was present the night of "Privacy II", a play I wrote and cast Max Julien in. Even before I took my first taste of the day, my nerves were beginning to unravel. What if nobody comes to the show. What if my investors lose their money, what if I do succeed and I don't find the answer to my souls yearning. Each question lead to another full glass until, I had enough liquid courage to pull it off.

Everybody who was important to the success of the newest ventures for The Punany Project, was there...Everyone watched as my inebriated tongue stumbled over lines that I had performed hundreds of times before. They watched as I nearly destroyed part of the set, in my attempts to use them to support my drunken legs. The artists who had been so dedicated to a project that could barely pay anything at all, became victims of my drunken tongue-lashings as I vented through wine induced tears about production problems that only existed in my head.

Dear Diary,

Friday, October 19th, 2001

If today were yesterday I could stop this queasy feeling of embarrassment streaming through my body... If today were yesterday I wouldn't have the shakes. If today were yesterday I would not cringe at the thought of my behavior last night. I would just drink until reality is gone. But today I admitted the truest things I have ever known. I don't drink for courage, I don't drink fun, and I don't drink to tap into a deeper well of art. I drink because I have to... Because, I am addicted... Because, I am an alcoholic.

Today is the first day of the rest of my life. And I will be sober enough to remember it.

Young, Gifted & Drunk
Running from My Success

My charisma could charm a serpent. My writing could change the world. My possibilities were endless. But my cup runneth over.

"Cheers," I held a glass out to toast the mirrors image that was a bloated clone of me. I contoured shadows on my face to thin it out. And prayed somebody would come get me from the hotel room before I finished the entire bottle of Chardonnay.

I can't say when drinking became part of my daily ritual. It used to just help me through some hard times. It used to just be a crutch from time to time to gain the confidence to get me through an open mic performance, a writing assignment, a dinner date, my monthly cycle, a Punany show... or for any other occasion I might find an excuse to drink. I subscribed to the strangest form of denial.

Pretty

"Oh she's such a pretty little girl."
"I'm a smart little girl," I was prompted to answer by my foster mother. Being pretty wasn't enough; being pretty wasn't even real. Most days I feel very unpretty. Most days I make myself very unpretty. Walking around the house and the neighborhood pale skin and fading red dyed hair, one may never suspect that I verbally penetrated minds and bedrooms across the world while fully made-up, seductively moving, scantily clad for the cameras of one of HBO's most sexually graphic and controversial documentary programs.
"What am I doing? A little voice in my head asked.
"Sex sells." I answered.
"Sales what?"
"I don't know. Anything. Everything."
"All I want is love."
"Then sell that."
"I'm no whore."
"Really?"

If I had been, I would have known how to make money with The Punany Poets. It would have been instinctive. But I kept telling myself that making money with it would make me a whore. But I couldn't stop working on the project. She was my alter ego. She was bad, bold, in-your-fucking-face. The stories she gave me were like a magic potion at first. But as the expectations increased, I began to be invaded by endless streams of thought racing through my mind, countless unsold creations rising from the ashes of a pile of clove cigarette butts. And all I could do was drink until the thoughts would stop and I could pass out. But my angels never stopped watching over me.

The night of the biggest show of my life I would learn why pretty could never be enough.

I was an alcoholic by design. As was my mother, her father, my father, and my brothers. And though I was raised in a non-drinking Christian foster home the juice was waiting for me to fall into its embrace and claim my birthright. "Come on let's party." "Come on let's relax." Come on drink the stress away." Sitting with a bottle and Billie Holliday crooning *our* blues through my stereo speakers, my painful memories became more and more real, popping out of my head and onto pages and pages and pages of the incomplete assignments of my life.

Smart

People always said I was strong, blessed, and gifted. Even when I was a little girl, the elders always said I had been here before, that I had an old soul. I became a writer before I could spell, building small stories and ideas into painful tales that could choke the heart into bleeding. My own life so full of pain and feelings of inadequacy about my color, my race, my poverty, my sexual deviance, ate away a big space in the center of my body. I needed to fill it. Like filling, then digging a grave.

I told myself I needed to hold on to my pain to become an effective writer. Notice, I say effective, not successful, an indication that I may have never seriously considered it as a real career. In fact, I left school, even after a young reporter offered to pay my tuition. What if I became rich and happy? Would I know me? Would I like me? And if I should be constrained to look at the world through rose colored glasses as my environment improved, what would I write about?

So what? Say I lost it tomorrow. What have I done today to make change? I know I have a purpose. I know I was called to speak to and for those who cannot or will not speak for themselves. And I'm scared. Petrified, that I might really reach someone. I might really have thousands of people who believe in me. I began to attack those who are already supporting me. Repeatedly sabotaging my life's work. I have missed planes for shows and business meetings subconsciously-on-purpose, drank my way through performances, insulted those in position to help me, procrastinated exceedingly, allowed other business to supercede my own and pushed away those who love me most.

Someone told me once that drink lips speak with a sober mind. I know the alcohol is only an enabler for the most detrimental part of my personality. I can remember being a child with high ideals. Don't you? Believing that I could and would do anything. And though I suppose, I have gotten further than many who lived in that life-sucking ghetto we cling to, I was infected with the inertia and ignorance that plagues it. The truth of my truth is that I am too fucking scared to believe in myself. To GOTdamed pussy to even *use* pussy to get myself a better life. (Damn it feels good admitting this, I'm even typing without looking at the keys.)

My foster mother use to say that poor black people act like they aren't used to having anything. My sister says the ghetto is not a place, it is a state of mind. I think maybe we just don't want to have anything more than what we are used to. Perhaps we even believe the bullshit we tell ourselves and each other that "to be successful you have to be white, or at least act like it". You know, the fear of the Uncle Tom syndrome. Whatever the case, at one point or another the elements of the ghetto are bound to get to you if stay there long enough. My testimonial, as Jessica Holter, the writer, the mother, the businesswoman is ready to leave the ghetto that has infected my mind. I will proudly don Punany's bootstraps and elevate myself into a new clear plain of not possibilities, but probabilities whose grassy meadow is nourished my a river of confidence streaming through it's center. And my friends, my family, my lover and my fans will fly with me.

Today I hold in the palm of my hand 1 completed manuscript AKA Dead Man, an urban mystery, The much sought after "Verbal Penetration", book an CD collection, a film on its way to the editing room, and more than ten collections of poems, short stories, song lyrics, music and art pieces.

AKA Dead Man, a story based on my childhood as a foster child and the daughter of an alcoholic mother is my true birthright. It is my piece of peace and the promise of a better tomorrow. In it's pages I will bury my grief and start whole, anew and sober.

Please enjoy the excerpt from my new novel "AKA Dead Man". If you are a family member, friend or fan, who has suffered because of my behavior, please accept the confessions herein and pray for my recovery from alcoholism and fear of success. I love you and I appreciate all of your support, patience and understanding.

Jessica Holter

AKA "Dead Man"

An Epiphany Brenner Mystery by Jessica Holter

EXCERPT

Chapter 11
Little Red Caboose

I didn't remember the trip to Jack London Square but I was good and drunk when I called Macio.

"Macio," I slurred, "come get me." I need you."

"Epiphany? Is it you?"

"Come on. I'm down here at the water. I can't take this shit Macio. I can't take rejection!" I screamed. A man pulled is wife closer to him as they emerged from the parking lot. I grabbed my crotch and said, "Fuck you God damned faggot peckerwood."

"Epiphany. Just tell me what's wrong, all right?

"I danced around in circles chanting "Ding dong the witch is dead—the wicked old witch is dead...."

"Epiphany I can't help you if you don't tell me what's wrong."

"Please come get me. Please?" I whined my voice was hardly audible.

"Tell me where you are........I'll be there in ten minutes." He hung up leaving me alone.

I had to pee so bad I couldn't hold it. I tucked myself in the corner of the phone booth and pulled my pants down trying to create an even stream that wouldn't run down my legs. I spread my legs far apart humming that song about the witch and rocked on my toes. I lost my balance and fell over before I had finished. A dark pink stain spread across the front of my sweat pants and made my thigh cold. The phone booth rattled a little and I heard a rumble. I tripped out of the booth to see....

"A train. A fucking train," I shouted. I ran up to the tracks a begged the train to go away. "Stop it. Go back where you came from. Go away train, go away caboose." I shouted at the mass of steal.

Blurry people stared, and milled around like idiots. "Stop looking at me, stop it, stop looking at me. Stop it! Stop it! This little black girl ain't for sell you honkies." I screamed until my voice wasn't more that pathetic whimper. My knees were on the ground and my head spun wildly as the pebbles in the ground got closer and closer. The street reached up and whacked me in the forehead.

—

I woke up in Macio's study. I saw a black mass of velvet fabric slip through the door and watched the door shut quietly.

My eyes scanned the dark wood paneled room looking for a hint of familiarity that would make me comfortable. Even in the strangest places I could usually find something to set my mind at ease. There was a fireplace that bore no resemblance to the one in my childhood bedroom, a bedroom Momma Owens had converted from a dining room. Macio's was brick, the smoky residue on its face indicated it was also well used. The brag pieces which stood on it's mantle, dotted with tiny bits of ash promoted memories of Momma Owens cheaply framed certificate, a constant reminder that we were foster children.

Macio's were professional credentials, a BA from Berkeley, a Master's from SF State, a framed clip from the Journal of Psychology and a photo of him with little children. Perhaps I stared at it for a moment too long.

"Inter-Race. Inter-Race Center of Psychology. It's here, In Berkeley. I founded it. Those are the kids from the first group," He said in a monotone I hadn't recognized over the phone.

"I want to help," he said, "but I need to know everything."

"I don't know why I called you. Thanks for coming to get me. I should go." I said trying to dismiss the pathetic actions that had brought me to this place.

"Well, Epiphany, maybe I can help you figure it out. Why you called me." Macio broke his sentences into to parts. Dissecting it somewhere in the beginning and adding the broken portion to the end as an afterthought.

"I don't know where to begin," I told him. I became ashamed when I realized how he must have found me. I looked down to see that I was wearing a plain blue dress and my hair smelled of head and shoulders.

"I found you were muttering, why don't you start there, with the train you were talking about?"

In my dream T'wana was hitting me on my neck with the pots and pans from the kitchen in my Head Start class. I could not hit her back. It was like I was stuck in slow motion like when Cindy had a crush on that boy on The Brady Bunch and ran to him real slow, even though she tried to run faster. And every time I tried to hit T'wana, my fists landed real soft against her head.

I heard noise in the kitchen that woke me up. Tiny Tim, my dog, had slept under my neck all night. I call him tiny Tim because he's like the little boy in the Christmas movie with the crutches that would never get well. My little dog would not get well either. When I got him for Christmas last year he could play music, all different kinds of music. When I walked down the hill with mother from my foster home and turned the buttons on his belly he played country music like my brother liked. I turned the button again and he played soul music like my sisters listened to, stuff like James Brown's "I'm Black and I'm Proud". It wasn't that song though. That was my favorite song, or at least that's what everybody kept telling me was my favorite song. When my sisters had meetings with their friends they would let me sing it for them. Then I would stay in the living room to here them talk about the revolution.

When I turned the little dog's button to hear the people talking about how Huey was arrested for beating up a black man, mother took the little dog away from me. She said "they" were trying to follow us. That "they" were using my little dog to track us to the free Church in San Francisco where we were going for Christmas dinner. I told her nothing was wrong with him. But she said she would fix him, make him loyal to me because I was his new owner.

She wrestled with him for a minute. I just looked down the hill thinking of all the bad smells in the Free Church and wondering why we couldn't stay and have dinner with Momma Ann and my sisters. Momma Ann had a big turkey with a lot of dark meat. She always lets me pick my meat first. The only time I liked liver was when she made her holiday dressing. Her dressing was plump with giblets and her potato salad was sweet with relish. At the Free Church I stand in line behind all the other poor people and wait for a small piece of dry white meat and green colored dressing with no giblets. The smell of people who had not taken baths in a long time or even brushed the smell of liquor from their breath mixed up with all the food smells until I felt sick. Mother always said that alcohol and free food was the diet of the poor and discarded. That Christmas, me and the little dog were as poor and discarded as the baby Jesus was on the day we were coming to celebrate.

Mother handed the dog to me. She put the little black box that gave him music in the pocket of her battle dress jacket. He was all empty inside. His brown eyes were still happy ones. He didn't know he was broken. I guess that's the way I felt about myself. I didn't know I was broken. I took the little dog from her and named him Tiny Tim. I decided, maybe I could pull some stuffing from one of my dolls and put it in his stomach. Now whenever tiny Tim gets sad and crawls under my neck in the middle of the night, I put a little more stuffing from my favorite doll into his belly. This morning I walk to my closet to find my doll but she is gone.

Mother is in the bathroom just outside my bedroom now. I can hear her shuffling through her medicine on the shelves behind the mirror.

Mother busts into my room in frenzy. Her feet, hard and cracked, seize the floorboards in my bedroom as she makes her way to the closet. She riffles through my clothes, grabs a few pairs of shoes and hurls them into my suitcase.

I don't need to be told to get ready. I arise quickly and dart into the bathroom. There is no time to bathe. I brush my teeth and pull my hair into a big fuzzy ball and wrap a rubber band around it. Mommy waits by the living room door. I know now that "they" must be coming.

Maybe this time I will see "them" before we leave. I peek out of my balcony window. I look to the street. It is quiet. Its dew is still undisturbed by tires. Perhaps they are hiding in the trees, protected from view by leaves and fog. Mommy often speaks of "them," but I can never figure out who "they" are and I never know when they will come. I never have seen them either but I am satisfied with Mommy's word that they are following us.

My suitcase is full of shoes. Her clothes are in a multicolored hand-knitted tote she wears strapped around her shoulder.

We walk for a very long time before she speaks. She says we are running away to New Orleans. I am glad. For her it is a quest to see the daughter she gave up for adoption a long time ago. For me, this is a chance to escape before we are dragged back into court for a custody hearing. I don't know where New Orleans is but I think it is far away. Far from the courts, the doctors, the police, social workers and "them." I wonder if Mommy knows them and ... Are they are friends with all the government people that keep telling me where to be? I want to be alone with Mommy so she can love me right.

We stop at the health food Co-Op for fresh ground peanut butter, jelly and bread. She drops the items into my suitcase. She walks fast and I am trying to keep up. Her thongs are run over, her heels are naked against the concrete that guides our fate.

At the Greyhound station Mommy gets me a coloring book. I insist on crayons from the drug store and then we stop in a dark bar with swinging door like the ones in the western movies. I sit by a window watching her promise the bar tender she would leave with me if he would give her one drink. He is shaking his head while she explains his own business to him.

"Do you serve food here?"
"Yes."
"Well then, you can't deny her the right to be here." It was decided.

From my window I can see train tracks. I love trains. For a whole year I have wanted a toy train with a shiny red caboose, but for my birthday and Christmas I got dolls, clothes and tiny Tim.

Mommy finishes two drinks and a conversation with a rust colored man with rust colored hair hanging off the stool next to hers. The morning fog has burned away. We face a sun brighter than the one we left outside the bar's swinging doors. Traffic quickens its pace and I am lost amid belt buckles, shopping bags and purses as she pulls me gently behind her. We are headed away from the Greyhound station, toward a big intersection. We are standing very near the curb at the AC transit bus stop before I can see again. I guess we will go as far as the city bus line will take us and hitch hike the rest of the way to New Orleans. The men we usually hitch hike with are truck drivers.

The trucks are big and I have to be lifted into them because they are too high to climb. They usually buy me something or feed me. Sometimes Mommy has to pay for the ride. She crawls through the curtains and they follow her into the part of the truck I have never seen.

After standing for a little while, I can hear the great rumble of a train on the track just across the street.

"A train! A train! Look Mommy, a train!" I shout. The people at the bus stop smile politely at me as I urge them to enjoy the sight too.

"I see it." Mommy said, patting my head. The train thunders by pounding the track chukka chukka chukka. The caboose chases close behind seeming to barely hang on, determined not to be left behind.

"Mommy the caboose!" I shout gleefully. I look up at her but my quick glance robs her face of any expression. The weary tracks shout for mercy as the last little red car spins across. There is a man on the caboose. I am amazed. Mommy told me people don't ride on the caboose. Why is this man on the caboose?

"Mommy there's a man on the caboose!"

"Shhhhh." Mother begs.

"But look there, is a man on the caboose and there's not supposed to be because you said that...."

"Shhhh, Epiphany." She insists.

In a flash the train had vanished dragging the caboose and the stranger behind it. The man in the suit standing next to us grabs his briefcase off the ground and walks to the crosswalk. I watch mother's hazel eyes, discolor in anger, fear or intoxication,

I couldn't tell which, follow him across the street into a phone booth. She glares at me with bulging eyes, the ocean glow in them distorted by the swollen red veins. I could see the California clouds through her lashes spread out like the Chinese interpretation of San Francisco on flip out plastic and machete fans as she stares into heaven like she's waiting for a sign from God. Her hand tightens around my wrist.

"It's all your fault!" She shouts. At first I think she's talking to God. "That man is calling the police on that poor man hitching a ride on the caboose. It's all your fault!" She snatches me from the curb into the street. My feet dangle beneath me, barely touching the tarred plane.

"Who wants this little girl?" She shouts. The skin of my armpit burns like it does when my sisters and I play Indian Chief. A trickle of her sweat works its way through the crease of her hand and my wrist. It crawls down to my burning armpit and evaporates.

"Who wants this little girl?" She gives me a couple quick turns as she screams at spectators. People gather like children on a school yard gravitating toward a fight, thirsty for excitement. Women with shopping bags and men with briefcases will talk about us over dinner tonight.

There are no cars, no buses, only whispers and the distant rumble of the caboose. The rust colored man with the rust colored hair peers at me through the window. A woman walks over to him, hands him a drink. He disappears.

Some people gawk shamelessly from distant corners of the intersection. Others peek timidly as they walk slowly past.

Some drag their eyes slowly across us as they pretend to look out for the bus.

I dangle before these fearful shoppers and gutless travelers for long minutes, barren of pride and power. Everything that is me is up for grabs, for giveaway like the stuff in the free boxes I get my toys from. Momma Ann told me about the auction blocks where black people use to be sold. Maybe these people are not surprised. Maybe these people remember my Black daddies. I think of looking cute to attract a buyer but not one of the White faces will look me in the eye. Not one spectator comes over to pull my lips back and check my teeth or separate the hairs on my head in search of mites. They just look down from their pedestals with the approval of silence.

Mother and I are an unlikely pair, so much the same and so much different. We are like my refrigerator magnets, no matter how we try to be together there is always an unseen force waiting to pull us apart. Like the social workers that flash seemingly innocent smiles, then, with a stroke of their mighty pens I'm shipped off to another place, there are always outsiders itching to tell us we don't belong.

"Who want's this little girl?" Mother continues to shout in desperation. "Who wants this little girl?" Her voice echoes then fades until I can barely hear it over the loud stares of the gathering crowd.

I look up at my mother trying to face her. If she would only look at me I can make her love me again. She does not look at me. She pokes her bottom lip out to blow her hair out of her eyes. She rocks back and forth, clinching my arm so tightly the pink of her knuckles whiten. Her toes curl up with drunken rhythm slowly tapping down on her run over thongs. She jumps at the sound of a woman's voice rising slowly above the assembly. The onlookers are surprised, like a secret meeting was interrupted. Like this savior was intruding.

"I'll take her." The woman said from a dusty white car across the street. Mommy pulls me onto her bony hip. She carries me over to the woman who hustles me quickly into the front seat of her car, and closes me in. She and Mommy talk outside the car behind the raised hood of the trunk. I stare at the boy and girl in the back seat, expecting answers. After a few minutes I realize they can't help me.

Sunlight creeps through the back window as the woman shuts the hood of the trunk. I embrace this opportunity as the last ever to see my mother. But she is not standing there to bid me well. I sit up on my knees to get a better look but I only get a glimpse of her battle dress jacket slipping into a circus of people, cars and traffic lights just beyond the railroad tracks.

***

The Story of Blue

Our strength is often composed of the weaknesses we're damned if we're going to show.　　　　　　　　　　　　　　　　　　　　　　*-Mignon McLaughlin*

A quote by Mignon McLaughlin, a 20th century American writer, faultlessly describes Jessica Holter (AKA Ghetto Girl Blue), at first sight, a small attractive California (ex)wife of a conservative Oakland police officer. A closer look reveals a loving and dedicated mother, a sympathetic friends, a compassionate writer and socially conscious activist. Look deeper into her dark brown eyes you will find her fiery soul, where abuse, neglect, abandonment and racism blaze a trail through a ghetto pandemonium from which the writer still struggles to escape.

When asked why she chose erotica as the platform upon which to build her spoken word family "The Punany Poets," she states simply, much the way her childhood rapist did in response to her begging of the question "Why?" -- "Because it was necessary."

"Somebody told me once, that the way to keep secrets from my people was to put them into books. Wondering of the truth of this, I decided to bring the poetry to life." I started giving little hustler sets with Dwayne Wiggins, recruiting writers and performers who could sing, dance, rap, act ... all around talents who believed in this sexual revolution, a revolution not of body, but of mind.

From the onset, the campaign to increase AIDS awareness through erotica was a publicity dream come true. Coining event titles like "The Black Whole," "Universal Piece" "Punany's Epiphany" and snappy campaign slogans like "Punany, even the word feels good in your mouth" GGB's quick rise to Bay Area popularity was not surprising. The project is *eclectically erotic: designed to stimulate, excite...educational: the promotion of safer sex... Resourceful: coupling with nonprofit AIDS awareness organizations-- lending a depth never before seen* in poetry, sexual abuse campaigns or spoken word.

When The Punany Project materialized on stage in 1997 it set the tone for the booming Bay Area poetry performance scene, encompassing all forms of artistry.

My poetry is simply the projection of my life," she says. As hip-hop reporter she often faced the degrading commentary of music men and as a front row consumer of after-show antics, the Death of Eric" Eazy E" Wright, chilled her to the bone.

"My life?... If I could give my life a name it would be "Irony". You know like a heavy Sakespearean play where the character tries to escape his fate, but each plan only catapults him closer to a predetermined end. It's scary when I think of it. Since I was a little girl, long before I ever discovered that my mother was beaten to death, I believed I would die at the hands of a man."

"Her East Oakland and foster family upbringing, along with the genetic heritage passed down from her Irish mother and West Indian (Black) father all combine to create what seems from outside to be a calm, Berkeley style, free spirited, compromising individual. That is until that deeper look reveals a creative energy and innovation that hits with the power of gale force winds, unveiling the existence of a presence with such magnitude that it could be housed in such a small package is itself a wonder.

Before she was born, her mother, "**Jane Therese**", whose name Ghetto Girl Blue uses in the controversial poetry collective , was a Berkeley hippie.

"My mother loved love more that it loved her. She met my father around 1967 and followed him to a beautiful nudist colony in Sebastopol, CA. Amid the tents and trees of Morning Star Ranch she was conceived. But before her birth, both of her parents were jailed for theft. GGB only knows of her father through the tall tales her mentally deteriorating mother told her of the "Black Jamaican Prince" with the gift of song and the curse of a violent temperament Jane came to expect in all of her black lovers

"Alcohol is a difficult vice to compete with. But when it is coupled with manic depression ... well ... she kept leaving me. I mean, at the police station with friends, until finally she wanted to go see her other daughter one day and just gave me away in the middle of the street....," a life altering event she recalls in '**Saturday Mourning**'.

A gifted writer, GGB's journalistic skills have been exhibited in Hipno, Huh, Roots, Urb, Vertigo, and 4080 magazines. Her work has also appeared in The San Francisco Bay Guardian, The Oakland Tribune, The Washington Post, The Community Connection and Urban 411 on-line Magazine. Her public speaking began in oratory exhibitions at the tender age of seven when the third grader encountered her first audience and "found her calling". "I studied in Toastmaster's International and the Dr. Martin Luther King, Jr. Forensic Society, primarily for the experience I planned to use in the pulpit."

Reared in the Baptist Church, GGB gained an uncanny ability to enchant the brother's and sisters with her prayer and sermon styled speeches, finding her words rising to the church beams and rolling over pews with a technique reminiscent of the late MLK. But her plans to minister soon came to a screeching halt when she was molested by her foster father only months after her mother's death, raped at fifteen by a man five years her senior and ridiculed by peers because of her impending promiscuity.

It was in her depressive state that she found Billy Holliday --

"I was thinking of suicide all of the time. Then Billy came to me, she taught me that I wasn't alone, that I should help people with stories of my pain and maybe some of the healing would rub off on me. I guess before I knew it I was back in the pulpit... Sort of..."

GGB's performance skills coupled with her literary gifts exploded to reveal a spoken word dynamo. Her unapologetic rawness in the GGB collective, a book of socioeconomic suffering and the abuse we lend ourselves to give and receive as well as her uncomfortably arousing erotica earned both criticism and praise; notoriety and scrutiny.

But the power of voice prevailed increasing The Punany Project to more than 15 artists of varied skill. Punany matured into a community campaign whose, in your face, no nonsense approach began to receive attention nationwide.

The new millennium will find Punany cocked and exploding with stories of love, loss and Bessie Smith/Billie Holliday reminiscent passion, as **HBO REAL SEX** spreads **"Punany: World Wide"** across an international stage.

It marvels me, how sex and pain fit together.

"It marvels me, how sex and pain fit together. A lot of people wouldn't be able to get through the pain without the sex. But when your salvation is deadly your troubles really begin," says the poet/journalist.

"When I was little I lived in a foster home with an apple tree in the middle of the backyard. In the middle of the trunk of the apple tree there was a gaping black hole with spider webs and dead flies in it. But the momma there, a big black woman, whose own pain shown on her face, made the best apple jelly of those tiny apples, born to die too soon.

Sometimes, when I'm doing the "**Head Doctor**," I see souls, hungry and longing to believe those words are real and personalized for them. That they are given of a black woman who harbors no anger about the slave time abandonment haunting us all, though so few are willing to exorcise those demons. I become the coffee in Bessie's Grinder, a potion in the gettin' up morning for Billie's black body hanging... And partake of the strangest of fruit."

GGB
Photo by Wiley Henry

Printed in the United States
25305LVS00002B/457-477